Educating from the Heart

Theoretical and Practical Approaches to Transforming Education

Edited by Aostre N. Johnson and
Marilyn Webb Neagley

Foreword by Paul D. Houston

ROWMAN & LITTLEFIELD EDUCATION

A division of
ROWMAN & LITTLEFIELD PUBLISHERS, INC.
Lanham • New York • Toronto • Plymouth, UK

Published by Rowman & Littlefield Education
A division of Rowman & Littlefield Publishers, Inc.
A wholly owned subsidiary of The Rowman & Littlefield Publishing Group, Inc.
4501 Forbes Boulevard, Suite 200, Lanham, Maryland 20706
http://www.rowmaneducation.com

Estover Road, Plymouth PL6 7PY, United Kingdom

British Library Cataloguing in Publication Information Available

Library of Congress Cataloging-in-Publication Data

Educating from the heart : theoretical and practical approaches to transforming
education / [edited by] Aostre N. Johnson and Marilyn Webb Neagley.
        p. cm.
    ISBN 978-1-61048-315-5 (cloth : alk. paper) — ISBN 978-1-61048-316-2 (pbk. :
alk. paper) — ISBN 978-1-61048-317-9 (electronic)
    1. Holistic education—United States. 2. Affective education—United States.
3. School improvement programs—United States. I. Johnson, Aostre N., 1947-
II. Neagley, Marilyn Webb, 1946-
    LC995.E38 2010
    370.11—dc22

                                                                            2011004753

∞™ The paper used in this publication meets the minimum requirements of
American National Standard for Information Sciences—Permanence of Paper for
Printed Library Materials, ANSI/NISO Z39.48-1992.

Printed in the United States of America

To children, educators, and parents

Contents

Foreword:

The Spirit Dimension of Education

Paul D. Houston

I once read a speech that Alan Alda gave at a medical school graduation. He ended by saying that he hoped the graduates would remember that "the head bone is connected to the heart bone." That play on words based on an old song says more about the role of the heart—and the spirit—in education than anything else I can think of. In the past couple of decades, education has been swamped by mandates that require increased attention to the "head bone," but there hasn't been the attendant emphasis placed on the heart and soul of education. Yet, as an educator for over forty years and a school leader for most of those years, I quickly came to discover that if you couldn't speak to the heart and the soul of the student, you were not going to get very far with the head.

Education is about motivation and creating connections. Motivation is found not so much in the students' heads but in their hearts. If you can get to them at that level, then you will bring their heads along. The mechanistic approach to school reform that attempts to address only the parts of the student deemed in need of fixing will not succeed. Education is essentially an organic enterprise where everything is connected to everything else. A holistic approach is required.

This book attempts to fill that vast void in current practice. It includes scholarly research showing why the heart and spirit of a student must be nurtured. It is also full of stories from the field where practitioners have been doing the difficult work of walking their talk. This combination of solid theory and practice must be attended to.

Most of my professional life has been spent as a school leader and as a leader of leaders. Naturally when I look at education, I do so through that lens. For our schools to become places where heart and head are in balance, our leaders must be intimately engaged in that work. It is difficult for teachers to introduce this balance in a hostile environment. So, at the least, school leaders must not impede the work. But for real breakthroughs to occur, real leadership is required. A principal or a superintendent focusing a meeting on the question of how we might do more to integrate the head and the heart in our schools would be a powerful beginning.

Most of the work I have done lately has been around the issue of spirituality in leadership. I think that leaders who are connected to that part of themselves can go a long way toward creating schools where the heart bone is truly connected to the head bone.

A number of years ago my friend Steve Sokolow and I attended a seminar for superintendents at Harvard. After listening to our colleagues sharing war stories of the battles they were facing in their work and adding our own stories to the heap of misery, we started talking about how we might face our work with a better sense of purpose. We quickly concluded that the causes of our despair would not go away; there would always be boards of education, demanding parents, recalcitrant workers, and impositions from state and federal governments. So change had to come from us—from a deeper place than we had mined up to that point.

That led us to discuss some of the reading we had been doing on spiritual topics, from folks like Wayne Dyer and Deepak Chopra to more esoteric and controversial writers such as Shirley McClain. We discovered that we found comfort not in the usual literature of school administration but in the works surrounding the spiritual side of the human endeavor. Since Steve was Jewish and my tradition was mainstream Methodism, we found with some surprise that we shared common principles and that, when we could stay in touch with them, we faced our work with more optimism and with a greater sense of possibility.

That realization led us to several decades of intense discussion that hasn't stopped yet. Steve continued his exploration of energy work, and I found myself infusing my speeches and writings with references to spiritual issues. We began work on a series of books. The first, *The Spiritual Dimension of Leadership*, was published by Corwin Press in 2006. This work also prompted us to establish the Center for Empowered Leadership (www.cfel.org), which helps leaders tap into the power of spirituality.

Delineating the difference between religion and spirituality is important. School leadership takes place in a secular environment, and the separation of church and state is a fundamental tenet of our culture. Think for a moment about pipes. We have lead pipes, copper pipes, and plastic pipes of every shape and dimension. Religions are like these pipes: Each religion has its own characteristics shaped by its belief system and dogma, but what flows through them is the same for all—in this case, spirituality.

Sadly, in today's world, religion has separated people and caused conflict and suffering. To my mind, nothing inherent within religion has caused this—it is merely a strong adherence to the idea that only one path leads to enlightenment and it must be walked with one belief system. This is not unlike the current trend we are fighting in school reform that there is only one way to improve learning—through a strict standards and accountability model. Yet I have visited countries in other parts of the world that follow different models to great success. The point is, many paths lead to the destination, whether in school reform or spiritual understanding.

Spirituality, on the other hand, isn't so much what separates us as what brings us together. Whether a Buddhist or a Baptist, the belief in trust or forgiveness is central. So when I talk about spirituality, I am talking about those things that bring us together as humans. To me, spirituality is simply creating a deeper connection to our most profound human aspects. It is also a willingness to reach out to others and join in the human dance that unites us. And it is the desire to strengthen that golden cord that connects us to our own version of the divine. A leader who is in touch with these concepts will be able to affect others in the organization to be open to them as well. And when the adults are open, the children can walk through that gate.

So why is this important for school leaders? And what might it mean? I get those questions often. I give a simple answer: As leaders we are called upon to perform complex tasks. Our success in completing those tasks has implications not only for our own success but for our organizations as well. For example, a leader must learn to delegate work. Most of us had training in that, or at least had to read about it at some point. However, it doesn't matter how much you have studied delegation—if you cannot trust and forgive, you will never delegate.

You have to place your trust in the person you are giving the work to and be willing to forgive them for not doing it as well as you believe you would have. If you are incapable of realizing those two principles, you will never effectively delegate, no matter how many workshops you take. You will micromanage your staff, annoying them and exhausting yourself. The fact is, leaders who fail to stay in touch with basic spiritual principles will never be as effective as they might be with just a bit deeper understanding of their work and themselves.

And central to all this is keeping our eyes on what is important. Certainly test scores and student achievement are the focus of the day. But what is truly important is the lives of the children we serve. We are the keepers of their possibilities. They need academic skills to be successful in life, but they also need human skills to be successful human beings, and that takes us quickly to a deeper dimension of our work.

As to why it is important, I think the answer is pretty basic. That despair I heard in the voices at the Harvard seminar is repeated daily in the education field. Education, while it has incredibly deep purpose, is fraught with pettiness and frustration. G. K. Chesterton said that education is the soul of a society as it passes from one generation to the next. Educators like to say that our work is important because children are our future. That might be true, but more important, we are their guide to that future. What we do today will profoundly affect the lives of our children, our communities, our country, and our world. The power of our purpose could not be clearer.

Yet, every day we are surrounded, as the cartoon character Pogo once observed, by insurmountable opportunities. We face the fact that as a nation we talk a lot about our children but don't really take very good care of them. Our ranking on such issues as child health, prenatal care, child abuse, and what-have-you puts us well behind the rest of the developed world. Educators sit at the vortex of our society's failure to care for its children. We know what their needs are, but are often helpless to provide for them. Yet, accountability is reserved for educators. Educators are asked to make brick without straw and to die for other people's sins. No wonder educators are frustrated and demoralized.

When I first started talking to public school superintendents about spirituality, I expected some push back. What I found was relief and great interest. I realized these professionals were hungry for answers and thirsty for a sense of support. What I said resonated with their concerns and calmed their disquiet. Several years ago, the American Association of School Administrators published an edition of the *School Administrator* centered on spirituality, and it was one of the best-selling issues we had ever done. People out there are looking for relief from their frustration and their sense of failure. Spirituality will not make you successful, but it will put you in touch with what you need to do to *become* successful.

It is no accident that one of the most successful book series in history is the Harry Potter books. While they are certainly not about religion, and in fact they have been attacked by some of the fundamentalist churches, the books are about the most profound spiritual dilemmas we face. They lay out the difficulty of good encountering evil and what it takes to prevail in such a confrontation. In one of the books, Harry and Dumbledore, the headmaster of Hogwarts School of Witchcraft and Wizardry, are having a conversation about success. Dumbledore reminds Harry that our success in life is not shaped by the talents we have, but by the choices we make.

I believe that one of the most important decisions a school leader can make is to find ways to tap more deeply into the well of spirituality that lies within each of us. Spirituality is an oasis in the desert of conflict and despair that makes up too much of a school leader's work in today's climate. The principles that swim there can strengthen skill and will. They can also increase effectiveness in working with others—the very essence of leadership.

Leaders get their work done through others. It has been said that managers do things right, and leaders do the right things. In our book, Steve and I suggest that empowered leaders do the right things for the right reasons. Working from that core, leaders can inspire and empower those around them. And throughout it all, we must keep in mind the connection between the "head bone" and the "heart bone," for it is in that connection that real achievement will be accomplished. This book will help you make that connection.

Paul D. Houston
Executive Director, Emeritus, American
Association of School Administrators
President, Center for Empowered Leaders

Preface

Marilyn Webb Neagley

In late 2004, when asked by the Ferguson Foundation to find ways of bringing the "spirit dimension" to adolescents, I joined with a group of advisers to form Talk About Wellness (TAW) as an initiative. Based in Vermont, the organization began by searching for existing programs. Although there were a number of authors and scholars who had begun work in this field, very few had reached the broad youth population through programs that were suitable for public schools, where the largest and most diverse population of youth are influenced.

Parker Palmer was one of the first to suggest that schools were missing this more spiritual dimension. Dr. Paul Houston, recent leader of the American Association of School Administrators and author of this book's foreword, had gained attention for introducing the "spiritual" theme within his organization. Linda Lantieri and others also began to express the need for "schools with spirit."

Social and emotional learning had begun to find its way into school programs through organizations such as CASEL (Collaborative for Academic, Social, and Emotional Learning), but it seemed that a deeper aspect of the "whole child" was missing. The Ferguson Foundation's interest originally began as a way of preventing high-risk behaviors, but soon grew into a belief that overall wellness, academic achievement, and social benefits such as kindness, compassion, and respect could be positively affected by working in a deeper and more heartfelt way with our youth.

The Vermont group's early investigation coincided with the 2004 release of *A Part of You So Deep: What Vulnerable Youth Have to Say about Spirituality*, a report by Melanie Wilson of the New England Network for Child, Youth, and Family Services (NEN). The report indicated that the at-risk youth population was hungry for deeper spiritual connection and identified many ways of making that connection, such as meditation, prayer, nature, art, friendship, music, and silence.

We believed that the best way to reach the largest number of diverse youths was to ask public schools to incorporate programs into their curricula. One of the largest high schools in Vermont, Champlain Valley Union (CVU), readily agreed to pilot a program. The Ferguson Foundation offered a grant to start a pilot project as well as help to improve the nutrition program and create a fitness room, indicating interest in the wellness of the *whole* child.

The pilot began with teachers leading exercises on the simple goals of breathing, stretching, and consciously creating "pauses" in the form of five or ten minutes of quiet. This was done through CVU's Wellness Program. Pilot teachers were sensitive to the importance of careful language due to the potentially controversial nature of the topic. It was important to reassure everyone that in talking about the "spirit dimension" or inner life of a person, we were talking about a part of the person, not a religious doctrine.

Peter Perkins, who had conducted many of the interviews for the NEN study, was hired to present ways of introducing this material to the teachers. His concept of the "whole self" appears as a chapter of this book. Tobin Hart, Ph.D.—professor, author, and cofounder of the ChildSpirit Institute—was involved in setting the groundwork with teachers and students. For example, he spoke to a freshman class assembly on the subject "What Is Your Calling?" Dr. Hart has also contributed to this book a perspective on the importance of inner wisdom.

It became evident very quickly that many students from the first high school pilot project appreciated the opportunity to learn how to calm themselves and "de-stress," as can be seen by their comments in this book's chapter written by members of the CVU wellness team, Sue Wood and Deb Higgins.

Sean McMannon, principal of CVU, suggested getting in touch with Dr. Aostre N. Johnson, a professor at nearby Saint Michael's College. Johnson had worked for thirty years in the areas of education and spirituality and had national and international connections to others in the field. With an endorsement from a school district superintendent, TAW sponsored her teaching of a three-credit graduate-level course for teachers and counselors, as well as a one-credit course for administrators. The basic precepts of her course can be found in the opening chapter of this book. The second section of the book contains chapters written by students of her course.

The next step was to offer another course to youths in a more rural area to see how it would be received. Johnson introduced TAW to Jacqueline Kaufman, an English teacher who was leading a high school alternative program. Her course, "Inner Practices: Deepening Presence and Interconnection in the Classroom," grew out of her master's thesis supervised by Dr. Johnson. The class was filled to capacity with a diverse mix of gender, grade, and subject interest. Her course illuminated the need for teachers themselves to be practicing this work before children can be expected to learn it from them. Kaufman contributed to this publication, along with classroom teachers who took her course and were willing to share their practices.

In 2007, TAW, in the course of networking with other schools, programs, and organizations, attended (at the invitation of Dr. Johnson) a Spirituality and Education Network International Summit in Malibu, California. We were joined by a Vermont school counselor, Auriel Gray. Colleagues from Gray's school district had participated in Johnson's previously mentioned course. We discussed the goals for TAW and the possibility of encouraging programs with funding.

At the summit, Gray attended a workshop with Linda Lantieri, founder of the Inner Resilience program based in New York City. Soon, the South Burlington (Vermont) School District, led by Superintendent John Everitt and with backing from TAW, had introduced Lantieri's program to more than one hundred teachers and counselors who were supported by additional trainers such as Dr. Anthony Quintiliani. The parents of that school district are also taking an active and enthusiastic role in growing this aspect of their children's education.

This preface illustrates how a small group of interested people can come together, promote an idea, and create a ripple effect. Many have given volunteer hours above and beyond the call of duty. Others have encouraged and supported this work through financial generosity. Our hope is that the goal of nourishing the spirit dimension or inner life of the whole child will become important not only to those involved more directly with teaching children but also to government officials, school administrators, parents, philanthropists, and anyone else involved in directing and sustaining educational resources.

The tangible benefits could range from improved health, by reducing stress and risky behaviors, to enhanced learning through improved attention and self-esteem. In relationship to family, friends, and colleagues, many of us know the value of a pause before acting under stress, the shift that is felt when softening our hearts in the face of fear or anger, the desire to perform when encouraged, the thirst for learning when there is meaning, and the joy of lighting the spark in another. We must address the need for those qualities and abilities to be passed on to our children in institutional settings and in sustainable ways. They have been missing far too long, and the price paid by society is far too steep.

As research emerges and the importance of "educating from the heart" is validated, we are hopeful that this deeper and more reflective approach will characterize the field of education, the concept of wellness, and the meaning of "whole child."

Acknowledgments

Deep gratitude is expressed to the following supporters for their generosity and vision; without their support, this book and the work it represents would not have happened: Ron Seeley and the Ferguson Foundation; the J. Warren and Lois McClure Foundation of the Vermont Community Foundation; Holly Johnson/Wind Ridge Publishing; the Mill Foundation; the Bay and Paul Foundations; the Binnacle Family Foundation; the Argosy Foundation; the Growald Family Fund; Lisa Steele; the Four Angels Foundation; the Wisdom Connection in close association with Wonder & Wisdom; Katherine Arthaud; Mary Abele; and Patricia Fontaine.

Thanks to the contributing authors of this book for their patience, dedication, and wisdom.

With sadness, the loss of Rachael Kessler is acknowledged, but her life's work is joyously appreciated and celebrated. Parker Palmer, Linda Lantieri, and other pioneers in this field are gratefully praised for all they have done and continue to do to lead the way. CASEL and other organizations or individuals such as Daniel Goleman, who provided a foundation for this work by introducing the importance of social and emotional learning, are most appreciated. Thanks also to Melanie Goodman and Melanie

Wilson of the New England Network for their respective roles as fiscal sponsor and researcher, but more for their concern with the well-being of children.

Elaine Pinckney, Robert Mason, Sean McMannon, Helen Niedermeier, John Everitt, JoAn Canning, Sue Luck, Judi Maynard, Sheri Rand, and Pat Messerle represent the supportive leadership of two school districts that piloted programs described in this book. Without their support and the commitment of many dedicated teachers, the programs simply would not have happened. School counselor Auriel Gray coordinated and propelled the effort in her South Burlington (Vermont) School District with an astounding level of commitment and grace. Working with her, Sonny Cassani, Anthony Quintiliani, Teal Scott, Ferris Buck Urbanowski, and others have provided valuable training, and parents Susie Merrick and Lari Young inspired parental and community support.

Saint Michael's College also played a significant role in making graduate courses, workshops, and talks available to teachers and administrators.

Finally, thanks to Pat Goudey O'Brien for her professional and gracious assistance with the editing process, Kristina Mann of Rowman and Littlefield Education, and Bethany Blanchard of the Rowman and Littlefield Publishing Group for their professional and gracious assistance with the publishing process, as well as the many who are unnamed.

Introduction

Aostre N. Johnson

What does it mean to "educate from the heart"? What does it mean to "educate with spirit"? An increasing number of people, including parents and educators, are realizing the importance of these questions. The volume of related books and articles published, as well as courses, workshops, and discussion groups formed around these questions is growing exponentially. However, within this array of valuable resources, there are not many that link theory with practice, and there are very few that focus on initiatives in school settings. This book represents a collaborative effort by many educators at levels from elementary school through university who are wrestling with these questions in practical as well as theoretical ways.

"Heart" is often used as a metaphor for the deeper dimensions of the human being, including the emotional, intuitive, and "spiritual." Various overlapping definitions of *heart* from varied sources include: essence, center of emotions, human feelings, innermost thought and feeling, consciousness, conscience, courage, or spirit. *Spirit* also is diversely defined in many sources; definitions include: the life principle, the animating part of a person, the underlying source of consciousness, vigor or enthusiasm, and inspiration.

Everyone has a different way of understanding these words, as do the editors and authors represented in this book. In a general sense, all contributors see heart and spirit as dimensions of being human where we can find strength, meaning, and connections, and where we experience deep reflection, caring, and kindness. In this book, heart and spirit sometimes also represent our intuitive, contemplative center, our source of creativity, and our "inner light," the consciousness and conscience that allow us to claim our full humanity.

Although a particular religion may be at the center of this way of thinking about heart and spirit for some people, this book is not about religion. However, it is related to the most cherished values of diverse religious traditions. As the Dalai Lama says: "When we talk about trying to promote a sense of caring or compassion, forgiveness and loving-kindness, these values are not particularistic: These values are important to all of the world's major religious traditions" (quoted in Glazer, 1999, p. 87). And these ethical values are critical to all principled people, independent of religion.

We are living in a period of massive cultural, social, and environmental shifts in the world. Wars, conflicts, global climate changes, and worldwide financial insecurity take a particularly large toll on society's most vulnerable members, including our youth. In addition, children are spending less time playing freely and less time in the natural world. Instead, they interact more and more with various forms of media, including television, movies, video games, Internet activities, and cell phones. While these may offer some positive benefits, it is increasingly clear that in many countries around the world, information-overloaded young people are becoming stressed and distracted.

Adding to this stress, the dominant educational systems are moving further away from heart-based, holistic orientations to teaching and learning. For example, in the United States, the high-stakes-testing legacy of the national No Child Left Behind legislation is subjecting children to increasing pressure and narrowing opportunities for authentic experiences in the sciences, social sciences, arts, and humanities. Many teachers feel obligated to "teach to the test," focusing on memorization and discrete, disembodied literacy and numeracy skills.

This prevalent educational atmosphere is severely limiting to many educators, causing them to feel alienated from the profession they chose based on their own love of learning, knowledge, and young people. Educating with heart and spirit ideally begins with them. As Parker Palmer (1993) says:

> We need to open a new frontier in our exploration of good teaching: the inner landscape of a teacher's life. To chart that landscape fully, three impor-

tant paths must be taken—intellectual, emotional, and spiritual—and none can be ignored. Reduce teaching to intellect and it becomes a cold abstraction; reduce it to emotions and it becomes narcissistic; reduce it to the spiritual and it loses its anchor to the world. Intellect, emotion, and spirit depend on each other for wholeness. They are interwoven in the human self and in education at its best, and we need to interweave them in our pedagogical discourse as well. (p. 9)

This book is rooted in the perspective that heart and spirit are deeply intertwined with mind and intellect and that education is most effective when it is based on a holistic understanding of human development, learning, and education. Over the last decades, a body of scientific literature has emerged that suggests that all learning is rooted in emotion, that emotion "drives" both attention and rational thinking. Without emotional connections, education becomes dry and meaningless. Human beings are most adept at learning and remembering those facts and concepts that are personally meaningful to them. In addition, our capacity for sustained, deliberate, "mindful" attention is strengthened by focused and sustained in-depth inquiry into and reflection on topics of interest.

Current brain research also indicates that educational practices specifically designed to calm and center people can bolster "executive" or rational brain functions, focus attention, soothe negative emotions, and counter flight-or-fight responses to stressful situations that, without intervention, may show up in violent or self-destructive behaviors. And finally, a growing body of research suggests that people learn best in an atmosphere that supports positive, caring connections among people.

Each chapter in this volume addresses some aspects of what it means to educate with heart and spirit. The authors' perspectives are based on a combination of theory, personal understanding, and actual classroom practice. The first section focuses more on overview and theory, the second section on actual classroom practice. Dr. Paul D. Houston's foreword, "The Spirit Dimension of Education," provides a holistic overview of its meaning. It also underscores the critical significance of the topic for school leaders; without their participation, it will be difficult for the ideas discussed in this work to move forward.

My chapter, "Developing Spirit-Related Capacities of Children and Adolescents," offers a qualitative research-based approach to understanding and educating the diverse capacities that encompass the development of spirit in seven different areas: contemplative, meaning-making, self-reflective, emotional, ethical, ecological, and creative. In "Supporting Inner Wisdom in Public Schools," Tobin Hart redefines knowing, knowledge, and education, showing how the deepest intuitive dimension of these is often overlooked and offering suggestions for its incorporation into schools. Dr. Anthony R. Quintiliani's chapter, "Developing Mindfulness and Emotional Self-Regulation in American Education," brings in the current critically important arena of neuroscience research and focuses on the problem of stress, along with the solution of "mindfulness practices," including emotional self-regulation, in educational settings.

In chapter 4, Dr. Ann Trousdale writes about nurturing spirit through literature, offering insights into how children's connections with their spiritual dimension can be strengthened through reading and discussing well-chosen literature. She also recommends and describes a variety of books for children and adolescents that are particularly valuable for nurturing the spirit. Rachael Kessler shares insights from her many years of work on the meaning and importance of "rites of passage" for children and adolescents at various developmental stages, including transitions into elementary, middle, and high school and at high school graduation and suggests models that support each transition. In "Paying Attention to the Whole Self," Peter Perkins defines *wellness* and explains its five dimensions, including the thinking self, feeling self, material self, community self, and spiritual self, and some of the implications of these for educating youth.

In the second section, Jacqueline Kaufman's chapter, "Deepening Presence and Interconnection in the Classroom," describes her experience teaching a graduate education course for teachers, focusing on encouraging their own "inner practices" and then documenting the changes this course brought in their own lives and classrooms. Teachers who participated in this class wrote the three chapters that follow.

Donald Tinney's chapter, "The Yogi in the Classroom," discusses how his ten-year study and practice of yoga—not only the physical exercises but also the philosophy and living of the union of mind, body, and spirit—has transformed his teaching of high school English. Sara Caldwell explains the impact of the course on her life and teaching. She examines the results of ten weeks of a daily contemplative practice on her relationship to the students in her own middle school classroom and discusses the positive benefits of using a simple form of meditative practice with her sixth-grade students. Joyce Kemp also considers the impact of this course on her development as a teacher and educator, offering examples of growth in her ability to be "present," compassionate, and appropriately assertive as a high school teacher and to create space for relaxation and reflection for her students.

My graduate class "Educating from the Heart" stimulated the next four chapters. In "Integrating the Spirit with Total Body Fitness," high school health and wellness educators Sue Wood and Deb Higgins explain the process their school went through to implement a four-week unit that incorporated mindfulness and yoga. They also give an outline of the curriculum and share aspects of its effects on students. Middle-level teacher Deborah Thomsen-Taylor then explains how she integrates self-calming and stress reduction practices into her middle school social studies classes to support students' yearly research project. These practices include time management strategies, deep breathing, yoga, stretch breaks, and visualization activities.

In "Teaching Children Empathy," elementary teacher Jessica Toulis shares a unit on empathy that she created for her fourth-grade students based on relevant literature and a number of engaging activities. She also gives examples of the positive impact that this unit had on her students. In the chapter "Counseling from the Heart," Madelyn Nash provides an elementary school guidance counselor's view on the importance of supporting both teachers' and students' inner lives in schools, fostering emotional connections, conflict resolution, mindfulness, and self-reflection. She also offers examples of activities she uses with students.

The last chapter is elementary school guidance counselor Auriel Gray's discussion entitled "Nurturing Children's Inner Resources." She reflects on her own personal and professional journey toward this goal and offers examples of activities and a categorized list of books supporting children's inner lives that guidance counselors and teachers can use. She also discusses her school district's engagement with Linda Lantieri's Inner Resilience Program, which offers mindfulness-based stress-reduction practices to both teachers and students.

The editors believe that these chapters offer readers not only diverse and thoughtful perspectives on varied meanings of "educating with heart and spirit" but also a variety of practical approaches to embodying them in classroom settings. We hope educators will be inspired to support their own inner lives in ways that are most meaningful and relaxing to them, and that the book will provide them with the motivation and knowledge to experiment with some of the featured teaching strategies.

We also believe that teacher educators who are interested in heart-, spirit-, and wisdom-based approaches will find the book extremely useful as a course text. It is accessible and appropriate for both undergraduate and graduate students. It could be utilized as a main text for courses focused on holistic, heart-centered, and/or spiritual approaches to teaching and learning or as a supplementary text for more general courses on curriculum and teaching. It seems critical for pre-service teachers to become familiar with these theories and practices early in their careers, so that their teaching practice is heart based from the start.

Finally, we think that the book will be interesting to parents and all caregivers who are searching for methods that support the intertwined development of children's bodies, minds, hearts, and spirits. We hope it will be inspiring and helpful to anyone who believes that education holds the power to help create a more just, peaceful, and loving world.

REFERENCES

Dalai Lama. (1999). Education and the human heart. In Glazer, S. (Ed.), *The heart of learning: Spirituality in education* (pp. 85–96). New York: J. P. Tarcher/Putnam.

Palmer, P. (1993). *To know as we are known: Education as a spiritual journey.* San Francisco: HarperCollins.

I

OVERVIEW

1

✛

Developing Spirit-Related Capacities of Children and Adolescents

Aostre N. Johnson

For many years, I have been exploring and writing about the multiple ways in which the spirit dimension of human development and its relationship to education are understood and practiced (Johnson, 1998, 1999, 2005). Rather than defining *spirit dimension* myself, I research the way others have used *spirit* or *spiritual* in relationship to education. I read published literature in these areas, which has increased dramatically over the last several decades, and also conduct an ongoing study of practicing school-based educators. In my graduate classes and workshops, I ask educators who profess some interest in this area to write about their personal definitions and understandings of *spirit* or *spiritual* and about how these impact their teaching and learning environments.

In analyzing these sources, I have found various distinct themes or categories of definitions. These include (but are not limited to) contemplative, meaning-making, self-reflective, emotional, ethical, ecological, and creative. Each category contains or implies a number of interrelated human capacities. The word *capacities* is used because its many subdefinitions encompass a wide range of human behaviors and abilities, including aptitudes, skills, faculties, potentials, duties, roles, capabilities, and powers.

In this chapter, I discuss the seven categories named above, each with a number of related capacities. Although I list them separately, they are really intertwining, and while some educators emphasize a single perspective or theme, others highlight many of them. The central metaphor common to all of the categories is connections. Each way of thinking about the spirit, human development, and education emphasizes differing kinds of connections with self, mind, and world. The capacities listed are suggestive, not exhaustive of the categories.

CONTEMPLATIVE

In the most basic sense, contemplative or inner capacities are at the core of all other human capacities. In defining *contemplative*, the idea of inner/outer is significant; inner experience is highlighted even when the focus of attention is outward. *Contemplative* and *aware* are often used interchangeably. Infants are born with a certain kind of awareness, the ability to experience reality globally with their senses and feelings, initially unmediated by rational categories. The challenge is to allow them to gain symbolic thinking without losing the fresh quality of awareness, as well as to further develop their inherent contemplative capacities.

Contemplative capacities include:

- focused attention
- awareness or mindfulness
- acute sensory awareness and engagement
- attunement to internal rhythms and ability to sense/calm physical stress
- a sense of self-transcendence
- self-reflective thinking
- meditative thinking
- intuitive knowing
- engagement in a form of meditation that increases inner stillness and peace, self-understanding, self-transcendence, and/or a sense of connectedness

Contemplative education begins with a focus on educators and their inner life and practice; based on this, they relate to students with intuition, presence, and awareness. They also create physical spaces that encourage quiet and solitude, consciously incorporate silences into students' days, and are comfortable with "wait time" or periods of quiet in discussions. In addition, they may choose to teach contemplative methods directly, such as concentration on objects, sensory awareness, observing thought processes, relaxation techniques, and working with the breath. They might encourage older students to learn about the theory and significance of contemplative practice in human history.

MEANING-MAKING/EXISTENTIAL

Human beings have an inborn tendency to seek meaning and purpose. The human mind seems to be structured to find meaning; the brain is, essentially, a meaning-making organ. Meaning-making is also the organizing force in human development. Feeling, perception, thought, and experience are all aspects of the human meaning-making context; more complex developmental levels emerge as we encounter, internalize, and make sense of new experiences in the world. In a larger context, seeking the meaning and purpose of life is a human tendency spanning history, cultures, and the individual human life span. It is the driving force behind religious traditions and the development of disciplines of knowledge. The ability to lead a life that feels meaningful may also be one of the most basic sources of human happiness.

Meaning-making capacities include:

- reflection on and questioning about the meaning of life
- attunement to the meaning of one's personal life
- engagement in thinking about the "big questions" in life, including the significance of personal life, life in general, and the meaning of death
- understanding the roles that religion and philosophy have played in human attempts to answer existential questions
- living with mystery and unanswered questions
- engagement in inquiry in the various academic disciplines, utilizing them as different tools for understanding life

Teachers who encourage meaning-making reflect on existential questions and think about the meaning of their own personal lives as well as their lives as teachers. They are curious about and engaged in the subjects they are teaching, understanding each discipline or area of human knowledge as a way of making meaning of the world and modeling this for students. To the greatest extent possible, they base curriculum on enduring human questions and concerns and on student questions and interests about themselves, the world around them, and the nature and meaning of life. They create classroom environments that stimulate curiosity and allow for in-depth exploration of themes and topics.

SELF-REFLECTIVE

Self-reflection allows human beings to look deeply at themselves, to reflect on their lives and understand themselves better—their motives, emotions, personalities, actions, strengths, and weaknesses. It supports the creation and attainment of personal goals. It centers on looking inward, questioning, and seeking greater and deeper understanding and awareness of the impact of thoughts and actions on self and others. Self-reflection strengthens the sense of identity, integrity, honesty, and purpose of living. It is impossible to imagine a well-lived and satisfying life or a highly functional society without thoughtful self-reflection, but it is increasingly threatened by the outer-directed and media/advertising-saturated culture.

Self-reflective capacities include:

- increasingly mature reflection and self-knowledge about motives, thoughts, and emotions
- assessment of one's strengths and weaknesses, gifts, and talents
- discernment of a sense of life purpose and direction
- understanding sources of personal inner conflict and working toward resolution
- an increasing sense of personal identity and self-respect

To encourage these capacities, teachers continually reflect on the goals and results of their teaching methods. They model self-reflection for students and encourage them to reflect on and assess their own learning styles and outcomes and to monitor personal learning and life goals. They create a safe environment in which mistakes are seen as learning opportunities and questions of all kinds are welcomed. Teachers encourage the use of self-reflective journaling and writing. They allow students to make significant choices in their learning about topics, books, papers, and ways to represent knowledge. They may teach learning style and/or multiple intelligence theories/approaches so that students can assess their own gifts and talents. They recognize and celebrate diverse student accomplishments.

EMOTIONAL

Generally, emotion is the affective aspect of cognition and is experienced as a variety of feelings. At its deepest level, emotion can be seen as the longing to experience and express the nature of being, the life force, in its many aspects. It is the key to connection between human beings, as well as between humans and other life-forms. Those who see spirituality as grounded in emotion emphasize its centrality to knowledge, wisdom, and relationships. Increasingly, evidence from the neurosciences points to the idea that emotion plays a pivotal role in all types of thinking and knowing, including both the rational and contemplative. It is also a key component of living a fulfilling life based on mutually satisfying relationships.

Emotional capacities include:

- emotional openness and fluidity
- a sense of wonder, awe, love, gratitude, and joy toward varying forms of life
- emotional engagement with the world, ideas, study, and work
- curiosity
- perceiving, understanding, regulating, and working consciously with one's full range of emotions, including "negative" emotions
- perceiving, understanding, and relating effectively with the emotions of others
- empathetic response
- a sense of connection and belonging in family, school, community, and other social groups
- faith in self, others, and world
- identifying and calming personal emotional stress
- a sense of empowerment and self-esteem
- emotional resilience, recovering from challenging circumstances

Educators who promote emotional capacities are engaged in their own emotional lives, working on understanding their emotions and improving their relationships with others. They model faith and hope in people and the world even in the face of disappointment. They are emotionally engaged with subjects that they teach. They nurture their relationship with each student and focus on the emotional climate of their classroom and school, fostering emotional connections between students. They are familiar with and encourage school-wide use of resources on emotional/ social capacities, resiliency, and positive discipline—those that emphasize direct teaching about emotions and emotional calming and control.

Teachers can encourage curiosity and engagement in curriculum by including variety and choice for students, allowing them to study issues that enliven them. They can utilize relevant texts in all disciplines and especially in literature that contains wise and powerful lessons about emotions.

ETHICAL

Ethical understanding and action encompasses principles, ideas, values, rules, and emotions related to how human beings should relate to each other and to the world. It includes the development of an internal moral code that governs behavior. It is concerned with the questions: How should we live together? How should we treat one another, including all forms of life?

The definition and development of ethical behavior has been a central focus of all cultures, societies, philosophies, and religious traditions. Current media reports continually relate stories about the breakdown of ethics and caring. More people are realizing that in this world of increasing mobility, conflict over diversity, and inequitable distribution of resources, ethical education is critical.

Ethical capacities include:

- developing an internal moral code that governs behavior based on character traits such as honesty, responsibility, and respect
- moral reasoning
- acting on a sense of responsibility for one's actions, based on values of justice, community, and caring
- respecting and valuing differences from others
- recognizing and resisting prejudice
- engaging in caring relationships with and service to other human beings and the natural world—a "relational consciousness"
- interest in understanding the causes of conflict in local, national, and global arenas and interest in contributing to solutions
- using conflict resolution techniques to establish peaceful relationships with others

There are numerous approaches to teaching ethics in the classroom. The central focus is on modeling principles of justice in educators' behavior toward students and in classroom structure, management, and curriculum. To develop ethical capacities, educators must be aware of their own ethical development and issues, asking themselves such questions as: Am I improving my communications/conflict resolution skills? Do I look for the sources of conflict within my own life—and for the solutions to them? Am I becoming more aware of my own prejudices, including the less conscious sources that feed them? Am I educating myself about the conflicts in the world around me? Am I aware of the ethical issues underlying the educational system I teach in?

In addition, students need other ethical models. Teachers can highlight heroic individuals with strong ethical values and accomplishments. Another approach is to emphasize and teach particular values throughout the curriculum, such as justice, community, caring, respect, and honesty.

Educators also create opportunities for students to engage in caring behaviors toward each other, teach conflict resolution skills, allow students to participate democratically in the decision making in the class-room and school, and encourage students to engage in discussions and debates that exercise their moral reasoning. Ethical issues and dilemmas are highlighted while teaching each discipline and topic. Teachers also integrate a multicultural curricular approach that goes beyond the surface and includes working for social change by involving students in service projects.

ECOLOGICAL

Ecological understanding at its broadest encompasses an interdisciplinary, holistic way of thinking about life, sometimes broadly referred to as *systems theory*. Ecological thinking honors both the physical *embodied* nature of being and the connected, interdependent, relationship nature of the earth and its life-forms (and potentially, the universe). This perspective emphasizes the understanding of sustainability principles, practices, and values. Rather than being taught as a separate subject, it must be integrated into all levels and disciplines so that anticipating the rippling results of each human action becomes second nature to youth.

Ecological capacities include:

- perceiving the interconnectedness of nature and natural phenomena
- understanding and respecting the way the body works and a human's physical relationship to the world and place in nature
- meaningful engagement with the natural world with all senses
- feeling a sense of place, a personal connection to a specific geographical area
- taking responsibility for and productive action toward attaining ecological balance

Teachers anchored in ecological education honor their own relationship to their bodies and to the outdoors. Ecological education begins with the idea that every action taken has a ripple effect, that all cause and effect is interrelated. It is anchored in nature-based experiences, understanding humans' place in nature as well as a sense of place, the personal connection to a specific geographical area. It also emphasizes the physical body and sensory awareness as the basis of experience and encompasses physical and holistic health curriculum. Ecological education includes an understanding of traditional indigenous environmental perspectives and practices in addition to contemporary knowledge about sustainability.

Young people should learn about the current ecological crisis in ways appropriate to their developmental level. They must be encouraged to

contribute to solutions for and productive action toward attaining ecological balance so that they do not become discouraged.

CREATIVE

In some ways, creativity can be seen as the ultimate capacity, because it
most differentiates human beings from other animals and gives them the
"godlike" ability to envision realities that do not yet exist and then bring
them into being. Creative experience involves discovering a form that appropriately represents and conveys the meaning of imaginative thinking.

We can be creative in any number of ways, for example, with words,
mathematical symbols, visual symbols, body movements, or human relationships. An experience is creative when it contains and/or expresses
meaning that is fresh and new for a particular individual. Creative or aesthetic experience and expression are natural to human beings; this can be
clearly seen in the inborn tendency of humans and other animals to play.

The evolution of knowledge resulted in the development of disciplinary thinking, with each discipline of knowledge as a unique approach
to symbolizing and expressing varied aspects of human knowing. Adult
"geniuses" in each discipline, from the sciences to the arts, speak of "playing" with ideas and materials. Increasingly, contemporary culture seems
to be leading to passive absorption of experience rather than active, creative participation. Creative expression in all of its forms is an antidote
to the depression and addictions that seem to accompany this passivity.

Creative capacities include:

- discovering and using one's personal gifts or strengths for the benefit
  of oneself and others
- playfulness and humor
- using the imagination to understand self, others, and world
- bringing a fresh perspective to situations in one's life
- acting innovatively in some capacity in one's life
- aesthetic awareness and understanding
- using a variety of forms to express ideas in all disciplines of knowledge

Teachers who want to encourage creativity in their students allow time
in their own lives for play and creative pursuits, and they approach their
own lives, including their teaching, with fresh perspectives. They offer
students opportunities for a wide variety of age-appropriate forms of
play, encourage playful exploration and experimentation with materials
and ideas, and bring the use of imagination into all areas of the curricu-

lum. They teach about the creative process underlying all disciplines and highlight creative individuals in history and contemporary life. These teachers look for and actively support each student's creative gifts. They also allow students to express ideas using a variety of intelligences and art forms whenever possible.

CONCLUSION

There is a dawning realization around the globe that many people and cultures are losing touch with their inner lives in this era of increasingly high-speed, multitasking, high-stress, acquisition-oriented ways of living—and that this is taking an enormous toll on all forms of life on earth. A restoration of these inner human capacities is critical not only for the well-being of youth but also for the survival of the human species and the planet.

REFERENCES

Johnson, A. N. (1999). A postmodern perspective on spirituality and education: Hearing many voices. *Encounter: Education for Meaning and Social Justice, 12*(2), pp. 41–48.

———. (2005). Diverse perspectives on spiritual curriculum and pedagogy. *Journal of Curriculum and Pedagogy, 2*(2), pp. 30–36.

———. (1998). Many Ways of Understanding and Educating Spirit. *Classroom Leadership,* 2(4).

2

✛

Supporting Inner
Wisdom in Public Schools

Tobin Hart

On her fifth day of kindergarten, the day after her fifth birthday, one of my daughters was given a short homework assignment in the form of a preprinted page that required her to circle two out of three objects that belonged together. There were six separate questions on the page, each with a different group of shapes. One group included a small green rectangle, a green triangle, and a red square. "Which two belong together?" She circled the red square and the green rectangle. When I asked her about this, she acknowledged that two had the same color, but she also understood that two of them had four sides each.

The next day at school, the assignment was returned to her and this question was marked incorrect. Obsession with the right answer misses an opportunity to see the question with more depth and from multiple vantage points—in this case, to understand that some shapes can perform certain functions. My five-year-old explained that rectangles and squares form "bottoms" of things like buildings, while triangles may form "tops," like a roof. She could imagine possibilities beyond and beneath the surface. This homework assignment is a tiny example, involving a tiny kindergartner in her first days of school, but it will happen again and again. This emphasis on the surface will miss the opportunity for something deeper.

FIELD AND STREAM

Education remains guided by an assumption about knowledge and knowing that suggests a "banking" model: Students are filled up with information and helped to develop such necessary skills as reading and calculating. This model gets a rhetorical upgrade in the information age as we think about "downloading" rather than banking. But the premise remains the same. The road to success is paved with amassing more and more.

This acquisition motif is also in harmony with the consumerist zeitgeist of the age. I certainly do want my children to know a good deal and to gain some growing skills, but, if information doubles every eighteen months, how can they possibly keep up? How can we? Perhaps there is some core knowledge that remains relatively stable. This is a reasonable hope that is translated into conventional curriculum goals. However, as valuable as this foundation is, we also know that innovation, genius, discovery, and creativity move under the surface and beyond the information given to create new knowledge and fresh ways of thinking and being.

At the same time, we also know that education is preparation to walk into a future not yet determined. The speed of change—technological, social, and environmental—in the twenty-first century makes this stunningly clear, from access to instantaneous global communication to giant buildings collapsing before our eyes to a hurricane that drowns a city. Rapid and unpredictable change seems to define these days and presumably those to come. How do we prepare students for an uncertain future?

Rather than metaphors of banking or downloading as our goals of education, upgraded notions on the nature of knowing may be more helpful to focus on in this century. From computing and biology to physics and neuroscience, we are increasingly describing how the world works with words like *networks*, *webs*, *fields*, and *streams*, instead of individual parts, bits, and components, reduced to their lowest independent nature.

The forward edge of technology isn't bigger computers, it's better networking—ways of tapping into webs of information. In biology, interactive field (Sheldrake, 1995) and systems (von Bertalanffy, 1968) theories are more complete than atomistic component explanations for understanding how biological organisms work, from cellular to social levels. In physics, field theories explain the subatomic world (e.g., nonlocal influence and electromagnetism) in a more satisfactory way than, say, Newton's description.

The flourishing field of brain science tells us we operate as a neural web, one that even networks with others, underlying our interconnection in the field of consciousness. This has come to be understood as a neurological reality through the emerging field of *social neuroscience* (Goleman, 2006). And as William James recognized, with just a little self-awareness we come to notice that consciousness itself does not exist as chopped-up bits, but instead as a constant flowing stream of experience. These terms and phrases give us some better descriptions about how education might match today's reality.

A banking metaphor of education is not wrong; we *do* amass information. But it is incomplete and inadequate to explain the sonnets of Shakespeare, the inventions of da Vinci, the declarations of liberty, or how to tackle the peril and possibility of the modern world. Information and skills help us to frame questions and to interpret and compare data and expose us to new ideas and ways of thinking—absolutely central functions, to be sure. But other qualities of knowing are equally important. This is why, in the work of great minds, we hear descriptions of intuition, imagination, intimacy, opening, and even love. The task of schooling for the twenty-first century is not just to load us up but also to *open* us up— that is, to give us the skills to open and expand the range and reach of the mind so that we can see more and more richly. As opposed to merely amassing more, how do we move toward attuning to fields of knowledge and tapping streams of consciousness?

INTIMATE KNOWING

The great texts of the wisdom traditions are often depicted as "living words." They are mysteriously described as being alive on the page. This is why in all of these traditions there is an invitation to reconsider the words or ideas again and again in order to see what light might be revealed. It is as if the words are encrypted and compressed. To gain access to the mysteries and reveal the deeper meanings, educators have to break the code. The process of deep learning in secular education is no different. While the emphasis has become bits and bytes, the biology text, the notes on the board, the text that is the person or situation in front of us, and the world as a whole are living words awaiting expansion in order to be more fully understood. Their richness and dimensionality already exists here and now, but must be decompressed to be realized.

A secret to breaking the code lies in *knowledge by presence*, which involves not only looking at the outer data but also opening into ourselves. *Presence* in this sense is eminently practical for learning and may be recognized by such qualities as nondefensive openness, flexibility of thought, curiosity and questioning, a sense of wonder, suspension of disbelief, leading with appreciation over judgment, an emphasis on contact over categorization, and a willingness to really meet and therefore be changed by the object of inquiry, whether a new idea or a new person. The code is broken, the words come alive, and the world is opened only to the degree that there is a corresponding opening of consciousness within us—a kind of *reciprocal revelation* occurs. In this sense, we recognize that *what* we know is intimately bound to *how* we know. And that deep knowing moves paradoxically and simultaneously both inward and outward.

Such knowledge by presence reveals the intersection of our individual depth with a more universal depth. The universe lies not only outside of us but also within us; the outside can reveal the inside and vice versa. Ralph Waldo Emerson (1968) knew something about this:

> In yourself is the law of all nature . . . in yourself slumbers the whole of reason; it is for you to know all; it is for you to dare all. . . . Man is surprised to find that things near are not less beautiful and wondrous than things remote. The near explains the far. The drop is but a small ocean. A man is related to all nature. (pp. 47, 46)

A more intimate knowing balances the objective and detached knowing that dominates education today with a participative, relational activity. Together they form a more powerful and well-rounded dialectic that opens the mind and, through it, opens the world.

LOOKING OUT

Intimate knowing involves a goal of understanding, but not just in the usual or more superficial sense of shared meanings—"we both *understand* that this is a chair." The word *understanding* means literally "standing among or under." This implies crossing boundaries inherent in "standing apart from"—the root meaning of the word *objective*—and moves toward intimacy and empathy. This opens the door to a richer perception that transforms information and, along with it, the self who perceives. As Buber (1958) says, "All real living is meeting" (p. 11). Understanding of the sort I am describing comes in the activity of meeting. Understanding requires a fundamental opening in knowing. Buber describes this shift as a movement from an "I–It" relationship toward one of "I and Thou." Understanding comes when we empathize with the Other, lean into the Other, and suspend our distant self-separateness for a moment.

The attitude and intention we bring to the meeting is the first key. Simple curiosity, appreciation, and nondefensiveness lead into depth and thereby the opportunity for understanding. This is a kind of "beginner's mind" that young children and wise souls seem to have naturally and is demonstrated when a child gets absorbed in viewing an unusual bug or the shapes of passing clouds with a feeling of awe and wonder (see Hart, 2003). If, on the other hand, the goal is to simply extract a bit of data for repetition on an exam, there is little chance for bringing the subject to life. Sometimes we do just need the bit, but in an age of information, that information is just a click away. Today's education can be for something richer and deeper.

This intimate way of knowing is as useful in science as it is in human relationships. Nobel laureate Barbara McClintock, in her exploration of genetics, described a less detached empiricism, one in which she gained "a feeling for the organism," that required "the openness to let it come to you" (Keller, 1983, p. 198). Note that the intimacy she describes was not toward other persons, or even mice; it was toward corn plants. She was able to deeply understand and break the (genetic) code through her "feeling for the organism" and her "openness" to really meet it. The world is revealed to the extent that we open to it. As a result, the Other is no longer separate but becomes part of our world and ourselves in a profoundly intimate way.

Like McClintock and Buber, naturalist John Muir understood that this intimate knowing opens us to the visceral reality of our interconnection with life:

> The sun shines not on us but in us.
> The river flows not past us but through us. (Muir & Wolfe, 1979, p. 92)

Intimate knowing leads not only to what the Greeks would call pursuit of the True, presumably what education focuses on, but also to the Good and the Beautiful. This is a profound clue that we are tapping into the depths of the world. When we empathize and really meet the Other, the object in front of us seems to stream with life, whether this is a history lesson or our neighbor.

Thomas Berry (2000) offers that this knowing moves us from experiencing the "universe as a collection of objects" to "a communion of subjects" (p. 16). An ethic of concern for the Good—how we treat one another—emerges organically from such communion. At a time when violence and virtue seem to be increasingly the responsibilities of schools, the valueless search for facts (the modernist goal of science) is balanced and brought whole with the addition of a more intimate way of knowing.

Beauty also emerges from this quality of knowing and serves as both an outcome and a portal. Beauty is cocreated through the quality of our presence. It reflects the quality of our knowing as much as it does the object before us. As we dive in, like a great naturalist, we begin to see more richness, more depth, more subtlety, and often more beauty.

Beauty takes endless forms: a perfect pitch in baseball, a meal prepared with special attention to detail, a perfect lapis sky, the deep peace of an infant asleep in loving arms, the elegance of a mathematical formula, the heart of our neighbor. Beauty provides a doorway, gate, or bridge inviting us from one state to another, enabling us to expand our everyday reality and respond to something that is both greater than ourselves and intimately part of us. By entering that doorway and opening into that communion, we are brought closer to the experience of the union between our inner and outer worlds, between the visible and the invisible.

Somehow beauty sends a "ping" into our own depths. We hunger for beauty; in and of itself, beauty is nourishment and a necessity. "Beauty," Dostoyevsky said, "will save the world." In a more intimate knowing, it becomes integral in our search for what is true.

Some time ago, my then fourth grader had science homework. She was to read several pages about the solar system and moon phases and answer in writing the questions at the end of the section. This is a standard and valuable way to practice reading comprehension and was intended to explore science. My daughter's book had pictures and explanations of the phases of the moon. These seemed abstract, a little over her head, and, in fact, I found myself unable to get much out of them. I glazed over, even though I enjoy astronomy. On the other hand, the moon looked spectacular that evening; what phase was it in? If she and her classmates had compared the sky over several nights with the book, they might have gained a real foothold in understanding. But instead, the assignment was to memorize and repeat only what the text was asking for.

She was instructed to "name four systems." She was simply to repeat what was written in the text (basic information recall, valuable but limited). However, the assignment entirely missed the opportunity for developing depth of understanding. We may hear that students cannot tackle more complicated questions until they have the basics, but the basics are understood when applied and contextualized. In this particular assignment, the concept of a system is really a linchpin for understanding the pattern of the knowledge. But what is meant by a "system" is not brought down to Earth. Why are the planets part of a system (i.e., exerting gravitational influence on one another)? Are there other systems that we can think of (e.g., your family, you and a classmate working on a project together, this class, the biosphere, the school)? What makes them a system (a kind of relationship that could be explored in class)?

While my daughter can copy the words "solar system," remarkably there was no explanation in the assignment that the word *solar* means sun. By going just below the surface, we discover that the solar system is a sun system and that planets are operating in a relationship to the sun because of gravitational influence. There was no time (I checked) taken in the classroom for any exploration of suns, systems, moon phases, or the sheer beauty of the moon. No mention or explanation of the solar eclipse that had just occurred. An approach that skates along the surface of information provides little time or support to dig in deep enough to make substantial and meaningful contact. Whitehead (1967) understood that "education must pass beyond the passive reception of the ideas of others. . . . The second-handedness of the learned world is the secret of its mediocrity" (pp. 47, 51).

What if part of her assignment had been to "hang out" with the moon for a while that evening and perhaps for the next few nights, just before bedtime? To sit alone in silence under the moon and simply take note of her observations, as well as her own experiences, including feelings and thoughts (e.g., curiosity, fear, convenience of the light, mystery, beauty, fascination)? Great learners find a way to meet the object of their inquiry, and they regularly describe their fascination, wonder, and deep relationship with the object. Educators invite fascination when there is an openness to direct contact with knowledge.

"Imagine traveling to the moon." "Write a story or a poem about the moon." "Make a picture." "What is the system of you and the moon?" "What poetry is there about the moon?" "What can we find out about the moon landings?" "How would our planet be different without a moon?" "Interview each other about your moon experiences" (Hart, 2009). Even a simple science assignment has the potential for more depth, intimacy, and a real foothold of understanding.

LOOKING IN

In addition to meeting the world outside us, we can meet the one within. Contemplative practices cultivate interior gaze directly. "Contemplation" here refers to an epistemic process—a way of knowing—that complements the rational and the sensory. Various practices are designed to quiet and shift the habitual chatter of the mind in order to cultivate a capacity for deepened awareness, concentration, or insight. While various practices are designed to evoke different kinds of interior experience such as creative breakthrough, heightened concentration, or compassion, they share in common a distinct nonlinear consciousness that invites an inward opening or expansion of awareness. Once again, this opening *within us* enables a corresponding opening toward the world *before us*.

In a very literal sense, these kinds of practices represent internal technologies of the mind. Just as we come to rely on external technologies from a pencil to a computer, these inner technologies may enable shifts in attention and physiological responses, optimizing our mind for the task at hand. Demonstrable effects on physiological *state*, which in turn affects emotion and attention and ultimately learning, are most clearly and consistently documented as the result of contemplative practices. In addition to stated effects, change over time in *traits* such as empathy, perceptual acuity, and anxiety level have also been shown.

Further, recent research suggests changes in brain *function* and even brain *structure* as the result of practicing these kinds of internal technologies (Hart, 2009). Something as simple as a moment of silence can help us pause and recalibrate our systems, useful for clearing the mind while we work on a problem or for consolidating memory following some study.

Silence also provides access to the streaming depths. In Persian poetry, the poet often refers to himself or herself by name at the end of a poem as a sort of signature. In five hundred odes, Rumi (1995) concludes with the word *khamush*—silence. In silence, in emptiness, in stillness, in the breath, we open to some deep place and become its conduit.

> There is a way between voice and presence where information flows.
> In disciplined silence it opens.
> With wandering talk it closes. (p. 109)

In silence, more subtle levels of being are sensed. Rather than an active doing, silence involves watching, noticing, or just being. In silence, we can begin to hear the beat of our own heart or the pulse of our passions more clearly and witness the stream of our consciousness. In silence, there is also room to listen to the voice of the Other. In silence and stillness, we notice what has always been there, but never attended to: feeling, sound, thought, habit, presence.

In and of itself, a simple and straightforward practice of mindfulness helps to develop present awareness. William James (1950) understood the distinction between the *I*—the part of us that witnesses or watches—and the *me*—the content of our consciousness. A practice of simply watching the stream of consciousness—thoughts, feelings, and sensations—without either pushing them away or clinging to them, develops a capacity for detachment (Eckhart, 1958). This detachment is described not as a distant objectivism that is heard in modernist science, but instead as an open witnessing presence. For example, rather than just feeling angry, such witnessing and detachment allows us to step back and notice—"I see that this is really upsetting me" and inquiring about it while in the midst of it: "I wonder what this anger is about?" This not only develops the potential for emotional regulation and impulse control but also develops interior "muscles" of reflection leading to metacognition.

Emerson hints at this developmental arc: "Our thoughts first possess us. Later, if we have good heads, we come to possess them" (Sealts, 1992, p. 257). In this witnessing or watching, what occurs is "a mindful reflection that includes in the reflection on a question the asker of the question and the process of asking itself" (Varela, Thompson, & Rosch, 1993, p. 30). This process "begin[s] to sense and interrupt automatic patterns of conditioned thinking, sensation and behavior" (p. 122). Such technology opens one to see in fresh ways, overcoming defensiveness and developing sensitivity, essential prerequisites for the process of deep learning. In addition, simply and honestly observing and tolerating our own reactions may also increase our tolerance for others, so essential for understanding multiple points of view.

A simple exercise can nourish the capacity for witnessing and presence. "Where are you now?" teachers might ask their class. "Take a few moments and just relax. Take a few deep breaths. Close your eyes if you are comfortable doing so, and tune into where you are right in this moment. Are you thinking about the day ahead? Rehashing some past experience? Caught in an emotional hangover about a situation with a friend or family member? How much of you is in your body? In your head? Floating outside you? Stuck in a painful nook? Just watch for a few moments; just noticing where you are and how that feels." After a few moments, the teacher might suggest, "Now take two minutes and share your awareness with the person next to you" (or in a notebook, or out loud to the class).

In a larger or shyer group, educators might ask how many were thinking about the past, or about the future. How many were worried about the day ahead? How many were in their head or in some other part of their body, or outside themselves? As a way of explaining James's notion of "I" and "me" or the idea of witnessing, students might be asked if they noticed that some part of them was watching and some part was being watched. This exercise could be extended, perhaps by parents, into a daily activity outside of class. "Where am I now?" might become internalized as a kind of personal check-in, inviting a simple ongoing practice of self-awareness.

Such simple and brief practices—and there are many more, as well as other types such as the use of poetry, body focusing, pondering, prayer, movement, various meditations, and so forth—are a starting point toward inviting "interiority" directly in the classroom (Hart, 2004, 2008). These may be thought of as experiments with developing lifelong inner technologies of knowing.

As students look within, they are developing capacity and sensitivity in the primary instrument through which they investigate their world—their minds. This heightened inner awareness helps them to notice, regulate, refine, and receive. The body becomes a resonance chamber as they learn to listen to it; the reducing valve of the mind expands and opens, becoming a conduit; interiority feels more spacious, allowing them to take in more of the world and tolerate more of themselves. In so doing, they become more aware and awake in the middle of their life and even in the middle of their school day.

CONCLUSION

How we know impacts directly and monumentally *what* we know. A detached, modernist, objectivist style that dominates educational practice tends to treat the Other—the world—as a collection of objects. A more intimate knowing balances the objective and detached knowing with a participative, relational activity that allows us to look within and without.

Our most sustainable and valuable educational goals have little to do with test scores. Instead, they have something to do with a balance between preparing young people for surviving and thriving in the world while developing their inner life. The greater the complexity and demands of the outer world—and these days are flooded with information and tangled with complexity—and especially in the backdrop of the previous century of remarkable violence and change, the more essential is our internal discernment, understanding, and ability to be present in the midst of streaming information.

This aspiration for education and for our children involves meeting the world deeply from a place deeper within. Jacques Lusseryan (1968), a blind teenage hero of the French World War II Resistance, captures just this paradoxical dual opening when describing his discovery that he could see in a new way after he had been blinded (ironically, in an accident involving the edge of his teacher's desk).

> I realized that I was looking in the wrong way. . . . I was looking too far off, and too much on the surface of things. . . . I began to look more closely, not at things but at a world closer to myself, looking from an inner place to one further within. (p. 16)

This is the goal, deep to deep.

REFERENCES

Berry, T. (2000). *The great work: Our way into the future.* New York: Random House.

Buber, M. (1958). *I and Thou.* (R. G. Smith, Trans.). New York: Charles Scribner & Sons. (Original work published 1923).

Eckhart, M. (1958). *Meister Eckhart: Selected treatises and sermons.* (J. M. Clark & J. V. Skinner, Trans.). London: Faber & Faber.

Emerson, R. W. (1968). The American scholar. In L. Mumford (Ed.), *Ralph Waldo Emerson: Essays and journals.* Garden City, NY: Doubleday. (Original address delivered 1837).

Goleman, D. (2006). *Social intelligence: The new science of human relationships*. New York: Random House.

Hart, T. (2003). *The secret spiritual world of children*. Novato, CA: New World Library.

———. (2004). Opening the contemplative mind in the classroom. *Journal of Transformative Education* 2(1), 28–46.

———. (2008). Interiority and education: Exploring the neurophenomenology of contemplation and its potential role in learning. *Journal of Transformative Education, 6*(4), 235–250.

———. (2009). *From information to transformation: Education for the evolution of consciousness* (rev. ed.). New York: Peter Lang.

James, W. (1950). *Principles of psychology*. New York: Dover. (Original work published 1890).

Keller, E. (1983). *A feeling for the organism: The life and work of Barbara McClintock*. New York: Freeman.

Lusseryan, J. (1968). *And there was light*. New York: Parabola.

Muir, J., & Wolfe, L. M. (1979). *John of the mountains: The unpublished journals of John Muir*. Madison: University of Wisconsin Press.

Rumi, J. (1995). *The essential Rumi*. (C. Barks, Trans., with J. Moyne, A. J. Arberry, & R. Nicholson.) San Francisco: HarperSanFrancisco.

Sealts, M. M. (1992). *Emerson on the scholar*. Columbia: University of Missouri Press.

Sheldrake, R. (1995). *The presence of the past: Morphic resonance and the habits of nature*. South Paris, ME: Park Street Press.

Varela, F., Thompson, E., & Rosch, E. (1993). *The embodied mind: Cognitive science and human experience*. Cambridge, MA: MIT Press.

von Bertalanffy, L. (1968). *General system theory: Foundations, developments, applications*. New York: Braziller.

Whitehead, A. N. (1967). *The aims of education, and other essays*. New York: Free Press. (Original work published 1929).

3

✛

Developing Mindfulness and Emotional Self-Regulation in American Education: How Neuroscience Can Improve Both Education and Personal Lives

Anthony R. Quintiliani

So many of us suffer from acute and chronic stress, both of which cause serious psychological and physical health problems. When such stresses occur in children and youths, they result in weakened physical and psychological health and underachievement in both social and academic learning. When stress exists in young people already at risk for psychological or physical problems, outcomes are far more negative. When parents suffer from stressful lives, they are less able to be present minded and emotionally supportive to their children. When teachers and administrators suffer from stress at work, they are less able to attend to, concentrate on, and support the psychosocial development of their students. Through the normative use of secular, mindfulness-based, emotional self-regulation practices, many of the problems noted above will improve.

DEFINITION OF MINDFULNESS-BASED EDUCATION

Secular mindfulness-based education includes open minds and hearts, inner peace, and gratitude. Stress exists, and it is becoming more severe among students in public education. Psychologists and educators have developed effective interventions of mindful education, present-minded attention, calmness, and emotional self-regulation in secular settings. Research suggests that the use of these skills in schools improves relationships, learning, and psychological and physical health. Such a shift allows calmness in the face of stress, compassion in the face of frustration, and understanding in the face of conflict (Chödrön, 2007, pp. 15–36, 79–83).

Jon Kabat-Zinn (1995) and others explain mindfulness in a very specific way. It is defined as attention to and awareness of our experience in the present moment without judgment and reactivity. Another definition of mindfulness is the immediate acceptance of present-moment experiences (thoughts, emotions, behaviors, sensations, and memories) as they are, without any attempt to manipulate or alter them (Shapiro, S.L. & Carlson, L.E., 2009).

A practice of mindfulness allows the human brain to respond in a more neutral or positive manner. A mindless and impulsive reaction expresses itself in physical tension, psychological frustration, unhappiness, anger, and even violence. The more people practice mindfulness skills, the less emotional reactivity they experience. Regular practice of mindfulness skills reduces psychological and physiological reactivity to stress and leads to improvement in emotional self-regulation. And with improved emotional self-regulation comes improved learning. Stress will always be with us; however, when students and teachers become more skilled in mindfulness practices, there is a greater possibility for calmness, compassionate kindness, and more effective learning and teaching.

STRESS IN AMERICAN SCHOOLS, FAMILIES, AND COMMUNITIES

Our country, our families, and our schools sometime run on stress. A recent national survey on stress (American Psychological Association, 2008) noted a dramatic increase in perceived stress. Approximately half of Americans experienced increased stress related to meeting basic needs of their families. About 80 percent noted economic concerns as the main cause of stress; this figure increased from the 66 percent reported six months earlier. For people over thirty years of age, the percentages ranged from 83 percent to 87 percent. Financial needs, health problems, job security, and housing costs ranked highest among concerns. When the growing fears of economic difficulty and potential terrorism are added to this reality even more insecurity, stress, and fear are the outcomes.

Americans in high numbers also reported deteriorating health and psychological coping behaviors related to increased stress. Among adults, 47 percent reported more stress than they felt the previous year. Physical and emotional symptoms related to increased stress include fatigue (53 percent), irritability and anger (60 percent), and sleep problems (52 percent). Other problems (less motivation, more depression, anxiety, headaches, and muscle tension) had increased.

Certain self-medicative behaviors also increased in response to higher stress levels. About 48 percent of Americans reported overeating or unhealthy eating in response to stress. Shopping, napping, drinking alcohol, and smoking cigarettes increased as short-term self-medicative coping mechanisms. Children and youths also pursued these modeled behaviors (American Psychological Association, 2008; Anderson, 2008; Martin, 2008b).

A key problem with higher levels of stress and self-medication is that negative coping mechanisms become conditioned—they become habitual. When a person self-medicates, the stress-related behavior (eating, drinking, smoking, acting out, etc.) reduces short-term emotional discomfort, thereby reinforcing the behavior through its consequences (a conditioning model). This positive reinforcement (improved mood) causes the behavior to be used again and again as a short-term coping mechanism. Negative reinforcement also occurs in self-medication as a person learns to avoid punishing conditions like anxiety, depression, anger, and cravings. Self-medicating behaviors do not improve long-term effective coping, health, or happiness, but they provide short-term relief and, therefore, become habitual.

These negative statistics on stress in America also involve parents and teachers who may participate in self-medicative behaviors. Of course, if parents and teachers are impacted this way, so are children and youths. The young follow similar patterns in coping with stress, and sometimes adults in their lives simply add challenges to the existing stressors. Short-term, self-medicative coping strategies do not resolve the sources of stress, do not provide long-lasting improvements, and do not improve emotional self-regulation.

These behaviors often lead to other health problems (addictions, obesity, stress-related medical conditions). Ample research and practice in American schools as well as in clinics (Goleman, 1995; Gross, 2007; Lantieri, 2008; Mayer & Salovey, 2007; Ornish, 1996, 2007) support a long list of adverse health and educational problems that are highly correlated with chronic stress and the improvements obtained through mindfulness-based skills. The negative outcomes are both psychological and physical. The list includes: anxiety, depression, fatigue, substance abuse, obesity, sleep disturbances, immune system problems, muscular tension and atrophy, adult-onset diabetes, cardiovascular problems, cerebrovascular problems, digestive problems, impaired wound healing, problems in stomach tissue healing (ulcers caused by *Heliobacter pylori* bacteria), fertility problems, and higher risk of infections (Gross, 2007).

NEUROSCIENCE ABOUT THE
BRAIN UNDER HIGH LEVELS OF STRESS

Neuroscientists have studied the complex basis of brain-based changes in response to acute, chronic, and traumatic stress. There are biological, psychological, social, and spiritual causes of stress and our response to it. The main story about the brain under stress is based on neuroimaging research and neuroscience theory; it includes competition for control within the brain that arises among interactions from cortical areas (the newer human brain) and subcortical areas (the older human brain).

The neocortex, frontal cortex, and prefrontal cortex represent our newer brain as far as human developmental history is concerned. These newer brain areas are associated with executive functioning (planning, decision making, problem solving, self-awareness, analysis, synthesis, interpretation, concentration, purposeful intention, impulse control, integration of cognition and emotion, etc.). These areas are negatively affected by autonomic reactions, while limbic functions include fear-based learning, emotional tone, and survival reactions. Stress reactivity stems from stressors that may imply subtle and direct risk or danger (Beaumont, 2008; Cozolino, 2002; Wehrenberg & Prinz, 2007) and limbic reactivity. Autonomic functions include fight, flight, and possibly freeze.

It is in this interactive, hard-wired response that the hypothalamus-pituitary-adrenal axis is activated for extreme autonomic arousal. The thalamus and hypothalamus (in the older brain) are engaged fully in, among other things, conveying sensory information up to the executive areas and down to the deeper older brain areas. The amygdala (older midbrain area), represent the seat of fear-based survival, emotional and avoidance learning, social emotions, and aggression. This brain structure overpowers and may bypass frontal and prefrontal newer brain executive areas.

Older brain area reactivity is faster than newer brain area reactivity, adding survival benefits in serious crises. The hippocampus (next to the amygdala in older midbrain areas) registers the various external and internal stimuli related to an immediate stressor, helping to ensure repeated human reactions to similar stimuli in the future. Conditioned self-medication and older brain reactivity collaborate to reduce effective emotional self-regulation (Amen, 1998; Beaumont, 2008; Lanius, Lanius, Fisher, & Ogden, 2006; Le Doux, 2002; Pissiota et al., 2002; van der Kolk, McFarlane, &

Weisaeth, 1996, pp. 181–213, 297–302; Wehrenberg & Prinz, 2007). When people experience severe stress, their brain responses tend to be far more physiological and sensory than cognitive/verbal, further weakening emotional self-regulation (Austin, 1998, pp. 158–167, 348; Le Doux, 2002). When severe stress responses become the norm, glucocorticoids/cortisol (stress hormones) may damage receptor cells in older brain areas, resulting in even more stress-related impairments (Damasio et al., 2000; Schore, 2003; Wehrenberg & Prinz, 2007).

A more pressing reality is that when reactive stress responses become chronic, brain plasticity may make it more difficult to intervene. Plasticity is the brain's capacity to make neural change and even structural changes related to repeated psychological experience. Typical educational interventions are often cognitive (newer brain areas); however, the dominant stress problem is in older brain areas. Therefore, consistent practice of more powerful mindfulness-based educational interventions (not only verbal education) that strengthen newer brain areas can better assist people suffering from stress.

THREE CASE STUDIES

What follows is a brief description of three people (two students and one teacher) whose lives have improved through the use of mindfulness-based interventions for emotional self-regulation skills. All three suffered from various forms of serious stress, and all three experienced decreased life functioning, reduced learning/teaching capacity, and anxious unhappiness. All three improved their lives by using skills noted in the next section. Of course, names and details have been modified to protect confidentiality and privacy.

John was a sixth grader who suffered from attention deficit hyperactivity disorder (ADHD) and periodic social anxiety related to feelings of not fitting in with peer norms. His family was high functioning and well educated and expressed high expectations for John. He was not doing well despite medical treatment for ADHD. He often presented strong anxious feelings, which he self-medicated with social isolation and withdrawal behaviors. Low frustration tolerance sometimes led to anger. John was unhappy. His case was referred to me by school staff members who were curious about mindfulness-based interventions and requested consultation services from me.

Ellen was a ninth-grade student experiencing high levels of stress related to conflict and turmoil at home. Her home life was so tumultuous (parental arguing and yelling) that she would sometimes experience anxiety attacks just before leaving school for home. She presented symptoms of acute stress and, some thought, an anxiety disorder. She had begun to self-medicate by drinking small amounts of alcohol to calm herself. As each school day moved on, her anxiety worsened. Her schoolwork suffered. She sometimes detached from others and isolated herself to hide her anxiety. Ellen was unhappy. Her case was referred by school staff who desired to learn and use more advanced mindfulness-based interventions with her.

Janet was a single, thirty-nine-year-old elementary school teacher who had a history of serious personal losses and cumulative traumatic experiences. Her background set her up for more reactivity to typical stressors, especially when they related to her self-esteem as an educator. Her work performance suffered, her experience of happiness was rare, and her skin condition acted up whenever she experienced extremes of emotional reactivity. She presented symptoms of acute stress and psoriasis. Janet was referred to me for consultation and training in mindfulness-based emotional self-regulation skills.

These three people received training in the mindfulness-based skills discussed below. All three improved their performance, mood, and lives. John learned to calm himself and reduce social isolation through the use of breathing and other mindfulness skills. Ellen learned to use cognitive flexibility and other mindfulness skills to reduce her emotional reactivity to parental conflicts. And Janet learned to calm herself down by using body scanning, moderating self-talk, and other mindfulness skills.

SECULAR MINDFULNESS-BASED SKILLS
THAT ENHANCE EMOTIONAL SELF-REGULATION

Now that we know our stress reactions are based on hard-wired brain systems, how do we help children, youths, parents, and teachers develop better emotional self-regulation? Secular mindfulness-based interventions may be our best approach. In 2007, more than seventy scientific articles were published on the therapeutic effects of mindfulness. Some of the outcomes included decreased pain perception, reduced stress (and anxiety and anger), improved motivation, improved interpersonal relations, and positive changes in health status (Ludwig & Kabat-Zinn, 2008). Jon Kabat-Zinn completed research to support mindfulness-based skills for stress reduction, pain management, and psoriasis, with emotional self-regulation at its core.

The basic skills for mindfulness-based emotional self-regulation are formed around the capacity to be mindful in the face of stressors. Kabat-Zinn (1995) noted that the starting point is to practice focused attention with complete concentration in the present moment without judgment.

However, when using these skills, we must be mindful that even very subtle judgmental behaviors (including negative self-talk, criticism, and muscle and tendon tension) and other physiological responses may signal loss of emotional control to autonomic and limbic systems.

The most basic skill training used in the three case studies involved starting people with calm breathing, sitting or lying in a comfortable body position, with their eyes opened or closed based on personal preference, and with an intention to relax (using the frontal and prefrontal brain areas). This stage is followed by calm breathing techniques (slower and deeper, counting breaths, visualizing the number as it is counted, sensing the breath entering and exiting, feeling the abdomen extend and contract, etc.). Sometimes, as a more formal, discrete practice, this breathing subskill of mindfulness-based emotional self-regulation is expanded into breathing therapy. Research (Van Dixhoorn, 2007) has documented that such skills on their own may reduce physical tension and mental stress. From these foundations, reductions in anxiety, panic, depression, and sleep problems may follow. When concrete training in breathing therapy is integrated into full mindfulness-based practice, reductions in anxiety, perceived stress, and physical discomfort have been documented (Jain et al., 2007; Lee et al., 2007; Weiss, Nordlie, & Siegel, 2005).

The next stage of skill training is more psychological in nature. When a thought, memory, emotion, or body sensation distracts attention away from calming the breath, people are told to simply label it (thinking, remembering, feeling) and turn attention back to calm breathing. At this point, it is very important not to track, link, associate, analyze, or evaluate the distraction. Skills must be practiced regularly, daily if possible. Practice is required so that when the calm relaxation response is needed to reduce autonomic and limbic reactivity in stressful situations, it can be achieved without great effort (Beaumont, 2008; Benson, 1975; Kabat-Zinn, 2005; Nhat Hanh, 1987, 2004).

Such mindfulness practices reduce heart rate, blood pressure, oxygen consumption, and, most importantly, stress response. Herbert Benson's recent research showed the relaxation response (applied mindfulness-based meditation) improved antioxidant and anti-inflammatory activities in the brain and body (Dusek et al., 2008; Martin, 2008a). Mindfulness-based meditation has been documented in both research and practice to reduce subjective experiences of stress and emotional reactivity in people suffering from serious medical conditions (Carlson, Spence, Patel, & Goodway, 2003).

Neuroscience research (Austin, 2006) noted mindfulness practices (intention, attention, concentration, and alertness) may strengthen frontal and left prefrontal brain activation (cognitive strengthening), thereby providing a cognitive and metacognitive component (thinking about thinking) supporting emotional self-regulation. Many of these skills have been implemented successfully in school systems (Lantieri, 2008; Napoli, 2004; Napoli, Krech, & Holley, 2005).

More advanced mindfulness-based practices that include multisensory awareness and processing may activate the whole brain. These skills were used in the one adult case study aimed at enhancing the effects of mindfulness-based practice sessions by activating as many areas of the brain as possible in learning. The sensory and motor (somatosensory) strips of the cortex respond to inputs from various senses, especially kinesthetic sensations on the skin or in the body. Visual inputs are processed by the occipital lobes, and auditory inputs are processed by the temporal lobes. The three brain regions activate when we are paying attention. Brain areas activated in practice over time become stronger neuronally (Beaumont, 2008). The more brain areas that are activated during practice, the stronger the learning will be.

Another cognitive-strengthening mindfulness skill is sometimes known as "cognitive flexibility." In cognitive flexibility (as used with Janet), the person intentionally cycles out of negative thoughts, feelings, sensations, and memories as they arise. As the skill improves, this intentional shifting moves on to replacing negative experiences with neutral and positive experiences. In some ways, this is the ultimate goal of mindfulness-based skills.

Mindfulness-based practices may also increase frontal and cortical control over subcortical reactivity. Using stress inoculation through supportive self-talk; recalling pleasant (substance-free) experiences; practicing gratitude; using thought reframing (from negative to neutral or positive); practicing distraction away from stressful stimuli; recalling multisensory (substance-free) positive memories; meditating; walking mindfully; practicing yoga, tai chi, or qi gong; and even regular repetitive exercise, all help people develop improved emotional self-regulation (Amen, 1998; Austin, 2006; Baer, 2003; Bishop, 2002; Kabat-Zinn, 2005; Ratey, 2008).

Now there is even evidence that mindfulness-based meditation may improve immune functions and left prefrontal brain functioning (Davidson et al., 2003). Normative changes in mindfulness practice, possible beneficial changes in brain plasticity, improved cortical control, and reduced subcortical dominance will help young people and adults improve emotional self-regulation (Ruede, 2005; Siegel, 2007; Stegge & Terwogt, 2007).

We also know that mindfulness practices, even regular rhythmic exercise, may repair neuronal damage in the hippocampus caused by chronic stress reactions (Amen, 1998; Ratey, 2008). Although all of these interventions will have positive effects, specific and age-related adjustments are required. Such adjustments include the use of age-appropriate language and instruction, allowances for attention span and baseline stress levels, duration of skills practice, and so on.

CONCLUSION

As with the three case studies here, practicing various secular mindfulness-based skills improves general functioning and may be helpful to children, youths, parents, and teachers in improving their emotional self-regulation. John's personal tolerance for his ADHD and his reduction in social anxiety resulted in improved emotional self-regulation and personal happiness. Ellen's stress and anxiety were reduced even though her home life had not changed. She is calmer and happier. Janet's acute stress and psoriasis improved, and with these improvements came better self-esteem and teaching performance.

Emotional self-regulation will help to reduce various reactive, negative behaviors and responses (stress reactivity, anxiety, social fears, hyperactivity, impulsivity, anger, and aggression). We owe it to our children, parents, and teachers to provide them with the best possible interventions and training we know. Mindfulness-based skills make up the core of these positive interventions (Baer, 2006). The mindful capacity to recognize, understand, express, utilize, and manage emotions is necessary for emotional self-regulation.

There is also a strong probability that students who possess mindfulness skills may improve academic performance. Although evidence-based inquiries into how mindfulness skills may improve student performance are now being researched under various categories of study, some support already exists, much of it from the basic validity of mindfulness practices. If a student is skilled enough to calm or shorten autonomic reactivity, fear, and stress responses, he or she will be able to utilize executive brain structures and processes more efficiently. When mindfulness is attuned to multisensory perception and learning (seeing, hearing, touching, etc.), more areas of the brain show neuronal activity; more neuronal firing suggests better learning capacity.

These structures and processes are important in school-based learning. Since enhanced attention and concentration are important by-products of mindfulness practice, it is logical that students' attentional and concentration capacities will improve their study habits and possibly recall of learned information. When fear of failure is reduced—as expected in mindfulness-based classrooms where student performance is not punished and where compassion is viable—student willingness to try harder and be less attached to outcomes may improve performance. Doing one thing at one time—paying attention in the present moment—should help students to improve academic awareness toward what is being taught now. All of these mindfulness characteristics can be expected to impact learning in positive ways.

REFERENCES

Amen, D. G. (1998). *Change your brain, change your life.* New York: Times Books/ Random House.

American Psychological Association. (2008). *Stress in America.* Washington, DC: American Psychological Association.

Anderson, N. B. (2008, December). Weathering the economic storm. *Monitor on Psychology,* 9.

Austin, J. H. (2006). *Zen Brain Reflections: Reviewing Recent Developments in Meditation and States of Consciousness.* Boston, MA: MIT Press.

Baer, R. A. (2003). Mindfulness training as a clinical intervention: A conceptual and empirical review. *Clinical Psychology, 10,* 125–143.

———. (Ed.). (2006). *Mindfulness-based treatment approaches: Clinician's guide to evidence base and applications.* New York: Elsevier.

Beaumont, J. G. (2008). *Introduction to neuropsychology.* New York: Guilford Press.

Benson, H. (1975). *The relaxation response.* New York: Morrow.

Bishop, S. R. (2002). What do we really know about mindfulness-based stress reduction? *Psychosomatic Medicine, 64,* 71–83.

Carlson, E., Spence, M., Patel, K., & Goodway, E. (2003). Mindfulness-based stress reduction in relation to quality of life, mood, symptoms of stress, and immune functioning in breast and prostate cancer outpatients. *Psychosomatic Medicine, 65,* 571–581.

Chödrön, P. (2007). *Practicing peace in times of war.* Boston: Shambhala.

Cozolino, L. J. (2002). *The neuroscience of psychotherapy.* New York: W. W. Norton.

Davidson, R. J., Kabat-Zinn, J., Schumacher, J., Rosenkranz, M., Muller, D., Santorelli, S. F., et al. (2003). Alteration of brain and immune functioning by mindfulness meditation. *Psychosomatic Medicine, 65,* 564–570.

Damasio, A., Grabowski, T. J., Bachara, A., Damasio, H., Ponto, L. L., Parvizi, J., et al. (2000). Subcortical and cortical brain activity during the feeling of self-generated emotions. *Nature Neuroscience, 3,* 1049–1056.

Dusek, J. A., Out, H. H., Wohlhueter, A. L., Bhasin, M., Zerbini, L. F., Joseph, M. G., Benson, H., & Libermann, T. A. (2008). Genomic counter-stress changes induced by the relaxation response. www.plosone.org/article/info%3Adoi%2F10.1371%2Fjournal.pone.0002576.

Goleman, D. (1995). *Emotional intelligence.* New York: Bantam Books.

Gross, J. (Ed.). (2007). *Handbook on emotion regulation.* New York: Guilford Press.

Jain, S., Shapiro, S., Swanick, S., Roesch, S., Mills, P., Bell, L., & Schwartz, G. (2007). A randomized controlled trial of a meditation versus relaxation technique. *Annals of Behavioral Medicine, 33,* 11–21.

Kabat-Zinn, J. (1995). *Wherever you go, there you are.* New York: Hyperion.

———. (2005). *Coming to our senses.* New York: Hyperion.

Lanius, R. A., Lanius, U., Fisher, J., & Ogden, P. (2006). Psychological trauma and the brain. In Ogden, P., Minton, K., & Pain, C. (Eds.), *Trauma and the body: A sensorimotor approach to psychotherapy* (pp. 139–161). New York: W. W. Norton.

Lantieri, L. (2008). *Building emotional intelligence: Techniques to cultivate inner strength in children*. Boulder, CO: Sounds True.

Le Doux, J. (2002). *The synaptic self: How our brains become who we are*. New York: Penguin.

Lee, S. H., Ahn, S. C., Lee, Y. J., Choi, T. K., Yook, K. H., & Suh, S. Y. (2007). Effective use of Medication-based stress managment program as an adjunct to pharmacotherapy in patients with anxiety disorders. Journal of Psychosomatic Research, 62, 189–195.

Ludwig, D. S., & Kabat-Zinn, J. (2008). Mindfulness in medicine. *Journal of the American Medical Association, 300*, 1350–1352.

Martin, S. (2008a, October). The power of the relaxation response. *Monitor on Psychology*, pp. 32–33.

———. (2008b, December). Money is the top stressor in America. *Monitor on Psychology*, pp. 28–29.

Mayer, J., & Salovey, P. (2007). What is emotional intelligence? In Salovey, P., & Sluyter, D. (Eds.), *Emotional development and emotional intelligence: Implications for educators* (pp. 3–31). New York: Beacon.

Napoli, M. (2004). *Mindfulness practice workbook for children*. Tempe, AZ: Scholarly Press.

Napoli, M., Krech, P. R., & Holley, L. L. (2005). Mindfulness training for elementary school students. *Journal of Applied School Psychology, 21*, 99–125.

Nhat Hanh, T. (1987). *The miracle of mindfulness*. Boston: Beacon.

———. (2004). *Taming the tiger within*. New York: Riverhead.

Ornish, D. (1996). *Love and survival*. New York: HarperCollins.

———. (2007). *The spectrum: A scientifically proven program*. New York: Random House.

Pissiota, A., Frans, O., Fernandez, M., Knorring, L., Fisher, H., & Fredrikson, M. (2002). Neurofunctional correlates of post traumatic stress disorder. *European Archives of Psychiatry and Neuroscience, 252*, 68–75.

Ratey, J. J. (2008). *Spark: The revolutionary new science of exercise and the brain*. New York: Little Brown.

Ruede, M. R. (2005). The development of executive attention: Contribution to the emergence of self-regulation. *Developmental Neuropsychology, 28*, 573–594.

Schore, A. N. (2003). *Affect regulation and the repair of the self*. New York: W. W. Norton.

Shapiro, S. L. & Carlson, L. E. (2009). (Eds.) The Art and Science of Mindfulness: Integrating Mindfulness into Psychology and the Helping Professions. Washington, DC: American Psychological Association.

Siegel, D. J. (2007). *The mindful brain*. New York: W. W. Norton.

Stegge, H., & Terwogt, M. M. (2007). Awareness and regulation of emotion in typical and atypical development. In Gross, J. J. (Ed.), *Handbook of emotion regulation* (pp. 269–286). New York: Guilford Press.

van der Kolk, B. A., McFarlane, A. C., & Weisaeth, L. (Eds.). (1996). *Traumatic stress: The effects of overwhelming experience on the mind, body and society*. New York: Guilford Press.

Van Dixhoorn, J. (2007). Whole body breathing. In Lehrer, P. M., Woolfolk, R. L., & Sime, E. E. (Eds.), *Principles and practices of stress management* (pp. 291–332). New York: Guilford Press.

Weiss, M., Nordlie, J., & Siegel, E. (2005). Mindfulness-based stress reduction as an adjunct to outpatient psychiatry. *Psychotherapy and Psychosomatics, 74,* 108–116.

Wehrenberg, M., & Prinz, S. (2007). *The anxious brain: The neurobiological basis of anxiety disorders and how to effectively treat them.* New York: W. W. Norton.

4

✝

Nurturing the
Spirit through Literature

Ann Trousdale

M y father loved to read, and he especially loved to read to his children. In the evening, we would all pile up in the big four-poster bed or sit by the fireplace and listen to wonderful stories: *The Jungle Book*, *The Adventures of Tom Sawyer*, *The Adventures of Huckleberry Finn*, *Minn of the Mississippi*, *Treasure Island*. There we would be, the four children and Daddy, together, yet each in our own imaginations transported into other worlds, living through experiences that lay beyond our own experience, often laughing but also facing challenges of courage, of loyalty, of integrity, of kindness or compassion.

It is not surprising that I grew up loving to read, nor that I eventually became a teacher of children's literature. I had developed a deep appreciation for what literature can do for a child imaginatively, emotionally, cognitively, and academically. My appreciation of the role that literature can play in nurturing children's spiritual lives came later and by a less direct path.

I taught for years on the elementary, middle school, and secondary levels before earning a doctorate in language education, specializing in children's literature. One day, I received a phone call with a request to write a chapter on the intersections of religion and gender for a book on images of boys and girls in children's literature. Initially reluctant to take on what would be an entirely new line of research, I did some preliminary reading for such a chapter and realized with some surprise how differently religion was treated in contemporary children's fiction compared to literature in the past.

Gone were the moralizing tone and didacticism. Prominent authors such as Katherine Paterson, Kathryn Lasky, Cynthia Rylant, M. E. Kerr, Richard Peck, Jane Yolen, Bruce Coville, and Stephanie Tolan were taking children's spiritual questions seriously; they did not patronize young readers. Religious practices—and practitioners—were examined through a critical lens. And while some contemporary protagonists found their way to a faith tradition, for others a comfortable and satisfying spiritual life was created outside it. I thought this interplay between spirituality and religion and how it was portrayed in children's literature represented an exciting and healthy development and agreed to write the chapter (Trousdale, 2001).

I knew of no one else who was pursuing research in this area, but at a faculty meeting several months later, a colleague casually dropped a flyer on the table in front of me advertising the Second International Conference on Children's Spirituality to be held in Haifa, Israel, that summer. I attended the conference and discovered an international community of scholars interested in this subject. The following year, the First U.S. Conference on Children's Spirituality was held in Atlanta, Georgia. The circle of colleagues broadened, as did my understanding of the nature of children's spirituality.

I wanted to incorporate this new interest into my university teaching and research, but felt that it was necessary to distinguish between spirituality and religion. My students are primarily public school teachers or young people preparing to teach. How might this topic be approached without violating First Amendment rights?

My own insights into the spiritual dimension of human life led me to consider that there are four primary relationships in the human experience: with other human beings, with the natural world, with our selves, and with the divine, or spirit. I discovered the work of Rebecca Nye (Hay, 1988) and, later, Tobin Hart (2003), who further explored and confirmed these insights through their research with children.

One of the consistent strands in my teaching is the oral tradition. Children are asking the same questions that human beings have asked since prehistoric days. The stories told by our earliest ancestors—those we now call myth, legend, epic, fable, or folktale—were developed to explore these very relationships. The earliest of these—myths—were told before formal religious traditions came into being; religions developed *from* these stories. Story predates religion. Story was developed to nurture spirit.

Why story? According to Jerome Bruner (1986), narrative is one of two primary modes of human thought, two "distinctive ways of ordering experience, of constructing reality" (p. 11): the paradigmatic mode and the narrative mode. The *paradigmatic mode* describes and explains phenomena according to categories that are related to one another to form a system. This mode of thought, which Bruner also calls the "logico-scientific mode," deals in general causes and is concerned with verifiable empirical truth. In contrast, the *narrative mode* seeks to establish not formal and empirical truths but rather verisimilitude, lifelikeness. In contrast to the "heartlessness" of logical thought, narrative "is built upon concern for the human condition" (p. 14).

The work of M. M. Bakhtin (1981) also provides useful insights. Bakhtin describes two types of discourse that human beings may engage in. The first is "authoritative," a type of discourse that strives to determine behavior, or "ideological interrelations with the world" (p. 342). Authoritative discourse is characterized by distance from oneself, a lack of dialogic possibilities, a lack of play, of "spontaneously creative stylizing variants." Authoritative discourse is static with its own single calcified meaning (pp. 342–343).

Bakhtin describes a second type as having "interior persuasiveness." This discourse does not necessarily appeal to any external authority but is flexible, with malleable borders. It is contextualized and can be related to one's own life. This type of discourse offers further creative interaction; it is open, unfinished, and capable of additional representation. Harold Rosen (1986) describes narrative discourse as having this interior persuasiveness. Contemporary authors who were writing about the realm of spirit for children had abandoned the authoritative discourse of the past and were offering children greater freedom to explore spiritual questions.

So how do we distinguish between spirituality and religion? Hart (2003) defines religion as

> a systematized approach to spiritual growth formed around doctrines and standards of behavior. Religions were generally inspired by spiritual insight and developed in order to spread that insight through various teachings, rituals, and rules of conduct. . . . The original seed of religion . . . is the spiritual. *Spiritual* refers to an intimate and direct influence of the divine in our lives. Spiritual moments are direct, personal, and often have the effect, if only for a moment, of waking us up and expanding our understanding of who we are and what our place is in the universe. (p. 8)

These are the universal, eternal questions; the "big" questions of life. Do they have a place in education? Some would argue that they are the *essence* of education. Yet many scholars and teachers in the United States today are concerned that public school classrooms are becoming so secular that the spirit of the child, the essence of the child, that aspect of the child's nature that asks the important questions of life, is being neglected or ignored. How are educators to rectify this situation without violating

First Amendment rights or stepping over into areas of religious belief best left to parents and religious institutions?

I propose that we rediscover the ancient art of story. Well-chosen works of literature that speak to the spirit dimension of children's lives provide an opportunity to explore such questions in ways that are not didactic, but that are relevant to the child and leave room for play, for imagination, for dialogic possibilities. An annotated sampling of such works appears at the end of this chapter.

How are we to use such books with children? Reading to children is one of the greatest gifts a parent or teacher can give them. Its benefits far outweigh the time the parent or teacher devotes to it. It creates moments of shared pleasure, it promotes a love of reading in the child, and it opens new worlds that adult and child may explore together.

Sometimes, when finishing a book, it is better not to discuss it with the child but simply, in the words of storyteller Betty Weeks, to "let the story expand in the silence that follows." With other books, teachers or parents might want to discuss the story. Here it is good to reflect on the implications of Rosenblatt's (1978) and Bakhtin's insights. If we understand that in entertaining the spirit dimension we leave authoritative discourse behind to engage the child's imagination, to allow for play, for dialog, for personal interpretations, so we need to leave behind the assumption that it is the adult's job to impose our interpretation, to make sure the child "gets" the point we ourselves see.

Two approaches lend themselves well to such discussion. The first can be equally well used by parents or teachers, with an individual child or several children. An approach called "godly play," developed by Jerome Berryman (1991), can be adapted to stories that are spiritual but not specifically religious in nature. In godly play, Berryman starts with an oral telling of the story accompanied by the use of tangible, manipulable objects representing figures in the stories. This has been a particularly powerful way to engage children in stories told to them, but Berryman's approach to the discussion that follows lends itself to stories read aloud as well. And while godly play was designed for use with children in groups, the questions can also be used with individual children.

After telling a story, Berryman begins a series of "wonderings," leading with such provocative statements as, "I wonder what part of the story is the most important part" or "I wonder which is your favorite part of the story" or "I wonder where you are in the story. What part of the story is about you?" (Berryman, 2002). The storyteller listens to each child's response, affirming it by perhaps repeating its essence, and waits for other responses.

Such an approach invites children to enter the story imaginatively; it honors children's personal spiritual insights while considering others' responses. It allows children to play with the malleable borders of the story and to relate the story to their own lives. In godly play, the children are later encouraged to extend this imaginative interplay with the stories through other artistic expression.

The second approach, called "literature circles," was developed for classroom use by Jerome Harste, Kathy Short, and Carolyn Burke (1988) and further articulated by Harvey Daniels (1994). In literature circles, small groups of children gather to discuss a book (or portion of a book) that they have chosen to read in common. The teacher's role is one of facilitator, turning over more and more responsibility for guiding the discussion to the students themselves.

In Daniels's model for literature circles, the children play a rotating assortment of tasks. One child is the Discussion Director, developing questions for discussion. The Creative Connector draws connections between this reading and other readings or experiences. The Artful Artist illustrates a favorite part of the story. The Literary Luminary selects particularly powerful or expressive passages, while the Word Wizard looks for interesting or new words. The atmosphere is informal and playful, but focused. Such discussions require listening to one another and responding to what one hears or sees, thus experiencing the bonds of community. In addition, these approaches subtly teach children how to discuss books in a thoughtful and mature way and expand children's interpretive powers beyond their own individual response.

Mary Elizabeth Moore (1998) describes narrative teaching as "relational teaching." As she points out, "sharing stories ground[s] people in their heritage and give[s] expression to their present situation"; it "binds people together even across ideological divides." Stories have the capacity to "enflesh social critique" and to give hope for the future (p. 131).

If educators and parents are to nurture that aspect of children that asks the important questions of life, the aspect that seeks to understand the essential relationships, they might well involve them with story. Whether they allow the story to quietly find its own place in the child's understanding or engage in open-ended discussion, they are inviting the child to explore the possibilities of relating to the natural world, to others, and to oneself in a time-honored medium.

RECOMMENDED BOOKS

Picture Books

Agassi, Martine. *Hands Are Not for Hitting.* Marieka Heinlen, illus. Minneapolis, MN: Free Spirit, 2000.
Hitting isn't friendly. Hitting hurts. How does it feel when someone hits you? When you hit someone else? Hands are not for hitting; hands are for saying hello, for making music, for helping, for building, for working together. The text and illustrations are inviting and instructive without

being preachy. The author includes suggestions to adults for reinforcing the concepts portrayed. Ages 4–6.

Asch, Frank. *The Earth and I.* **Orlando, FL: Voyager Books, 1994.**
A child describes his friendship with the Earth: he and the Earth go for walks together, play together, sing together, dance for one another, speak and listen to one another. Ages 2–4.

Bang, Molly. *When Sophie Gets Angry—Really, Really Angry.* **New York: Scholastic, 1999.**
Sophie becomes angry when she must relinquish a toy she has been playing with to her sister. Her anger mounts to an uncontrollable rage, and she runs and runs to a special tree and climbs it. In its branches, she feels the breeze and watches water and waves until "the wide world comforts her." Her equanimity restored, she returns to her home, where her family is waiting for her and "everything's back together again." A familiar emotion is treated as a natural part of life, one that the natural world can bring into peace and harmony. Ages 4–6.

Baylor, Byrd, and Peter Parnall. *The Other Way to Listen.* **New York: Charles Scribner's Sons, 1978.**
"I used to know an old man who could walk by any cornfield and hear the corn singing. 'Teach me,' I'd say when we'd passed on by. 'Just tell me how you learned to hear that corn.' And he'd say, 'It takes a lot of practice. You can't be in a hurry.'" The old man could also hear windflower seeds burst open and a rock murmur good things to a lizard. When, one sunrise, our young protagonist finally hears the hills singing, it seems like the oldest and most natural thing in the world. Told in spare poetic style, *The Other Way to Listen* makes intimacy with the Earth indeed seem normal and natural. Ages 6–9.

Berenstain, Stan, and Jan Berenstain. *The Berenstain Bears and the Big Question.* **New York: Random House, 1999.**
The Berenstains have written many books on spiritual/ethical issues. In this one, the young bears ask "big questions"—questions that are not always easy to answer—and it turns out that these hard-to-answer questions themselves come from the Creator. A hint at a Judeo-Christian tradition, but it is not made explicit. Ages 4–6.

Bruchac, Joseph. *Between Earth and Sky: Legends of Native American Sacred Places.* **Thomas Locker, illus. San Diego: Harcourt Brace & Co., 1996.**
Little Turtle receives teachings from his uncle Old Bear about the many places in North America that are sacred to Native American peoples. Deriv-

ing from ten Native tribes, some of the sacred places are related to creation stories, some to sacred ceremonies, and some contain universal lessons about human nature. All speak of respect for the Earth and the importance of sacred places above, below, about, and within us. Ages 8 and up.

Cherry, Lynne. *The Great Kapok Tree: A Tale of the Amazon Rain Forest.* **San Diego: Harcourt Brace Jovanovich, 1990.**
A man is assigned to cut down a kapok tree in the Amazon rain forest. After a few blows, the man grows tired and sits down to rest at the foot of the tree. He falls asleep, and the various animals whose lives depend on the tree come to speak in his ear, telling him of the consequences to their lives should the tree be cut down. Ages 6–8.

Curtis, Jamie Lee. *I'm Gonna Like Me: Letting Off a Little Self-Esteem.* **Lee Cornell, illus. San Francisco: Joanna Cotler Books, 2002.**
In humorous rhymed verse, the alternating first-person narrators declare self-acceptance throughout all of life's ups and downs. Ages 4–8.

Demi. *The Empty Pot.* **New York: Henry Holt, 1990.**
A Chinese emperor is looking for a worthy successor. The young contestants think that the test he gives them is one of successful gardening, and when the seeds the Emperor provides do not sprout, they substitute growing plants. Only one lad returns with an empty pot—and learns that the real test was honesty. Ages 6 and up.

Dr. Seuss. "The Sneeches." In *The Sneeches and Other Stories.* **New York: Random House, 1961.**
The Star-Belly Sneeches lord over Sneeches who have no stars "upon thars." Sylvester McMonkey McBean arrives with a device to put stars upon the plain Sneeches for a price—which they gladly pay. Now the Star-Belly Sneeches have no markings of superiority, so they pay McBean to remove their stars. Back and forth they go, "Off again! On again!" until all the Sneeches have paid McBean all their money. They finally learn that "Sneeches are Sneeches / and no kind of Sneech is the best on the beaches." Ages 6–8.

Havill, Juanita. *Jamaica's Find.* **Anne Sibley O'Brien, illus. Boston: Houghton Mifflin, 1986.**
One day in the park, Jamaica finds a stuffed dog "worn from hugging" lying on the ground. Instead of turning it in to the Lost and Found, she takes it home, wanting to keep it. Her mother points out that it probably belongs to a little girl just like Jamaica. Jamaica has to make a decision, and is ultimately able to reunite the dog with his owner. Ages 3–6.

The Hunter: A Chinese Folktale. **Retold by Mary Casanova. Ed Young, illus. New York: Atheneum Books for Young Readers, 2000.**
A hunter saves a snake from death and is rewarded with the gift of understanding the language of animals. There is one interdiction: if the hunter reveals the secret of his gift, he will be turned to stone. From the animals, the hunter learns of an impending disaster for his people. The people refuse to believe him, and the hunter must choose between saving them and saving his own life. A powerful story of self-sacrifice and the need to attend to the wisdom of others. Ages 8 and up.

Lemieux, Michele. *Stormy Night.* **Niagara Falls, NY: Kids Can Press, 1999.**
A captivating book about a child's nighttime thoughts and questions: Where do we come from? Who decided what the first human would look like? Who am I? Is my whole life already worked out in advance, or will I have to find my way all by myself? I'm afraid that nobody loves me! Are things better after death than in life? The book ends on a peaceful and hopeful note. Charmingly illustrated in pen and ink by the author. Ages 10 and up.

Le Tord, Bijou. *The Deep Blue Sea.* **New York: Orchard Books, 1990.**
A creation story for a very young child, told in a simple, appealing, and assuring way. Its only suggestion of sectarian roots is the statement that God "saw that it was all good," echoing the first account of creation in Genesis. Ages 2–4.

Lucado, Max. *You Are Special.* **Sergio Martinez, illus. Wheaton, IL: Crossway Books, 1997.**
Punchinello was a Wemmick of very low esteem—in his own eyes and in the eyes of the other Wemmicks. One day he met Lucia, who was not like the other carved wooden people. Neither their praise nor their criticism had any impact on her at all. She explains her secret to Punchinello: every day she goes to see Eli, the woodcarver, and sits with him in his workshop. Eli welcomes Punchinello and assures him what others think doesn't matter—that he is special because Eli made him. He invites Punchinello to come to visit him every day to see how much he cares for him. As Punchinello accepts what Eli says, the stigma of others' criticism begins to fall away. Ages 4–8.

Ness, Evaline. *Sam, Bangs, and Moonshine.* **New York: Henry Holt, 1966.**
Sam, left with only her cat Bangs for company when her father goes to work, lets her imagination run wild. She learns the difference between "real" and "moonshine" when young Thomas believes one of her more

outrageous fantasies and as a consequence is very nearly drowned. A Caldecott Award winner. Ages 6–8.

Radunsky, Vladimir. *What Does Peace Feel Like?* **New York: Atheneum Books for Young Readers, 2004.**
Radunsky uses children's own words to describe what peace feels like, smells like, looks like, sounds and tastes like. Words for peace in almost 200 languages are listed in the end pages. An excellent stimulus for discussion. Ages 5–9.

The Story of Jumping Mouse: A Native American Legend. **Retold by John Steptoe. New York: Scholastic, 1993.**
Jumping Mouse has a dream: to see the far-off land. Helped on his way by Magic Frog, Jumping Mouse learns the value of friendship, self-sacrifice, and hope. Ages 6 and up.

Williams, Margery. *The Velveteen Rabbit, or, How Toys Become Real.* **New York: Henry Holt, 1983.**
A toy rabbit learns the value of love and of being loved. Slightly sentimental, but a great favorite. This classic story has been published in many editions, with several illustrators. Ages 6–8.

Novels

Burnett, Frances Hodgson. *The Secret Garden.* **New York: HarperCollins, 1911.**
A long-neglected hidden garden becomes a source of healing—physically, emotionally, and spiritually—for a crippled boy, an orphaned girl, and a grieving father. The young boy Dickon, never having broken connection with the Earth, serves as guide, as guru, as source of wisdom. Ages 9–12.

Fleischman, Paul. *Seedfolks.* **New York: HarperTrophy, 1997.**
A community garden in a poor section of Cleveland, Ohio, provides the opportunity for connection and reconnection with the natural world for a diverse community of urban dwellers. Told through separate but overlapping stories, Fleischman's young adult novel illustrates how a garden may become a site for personal and communal transformation and renewal. Ages 10 and up.

Hesse, Hermann. *Siddhartha.* **1922. New York: Penguin, 1999.**
After years of spiritual wanderings that do not lead to the happiness he seeks, Siddhartha comes to live beside the river with Vasudeva, a ferryman. As the river passes through the seasons of the year, and as he reflects

upon the cycles of the water from vapor to rain to source to brook to river, Siddhartha comes to terms with his own life cycles in a sacred journey toward the Divine. Originally intended for an adult audience, *Siddhartha* has come to be read by young adult audiences as well. Ages 12 and up.

Hesse, Karen. *A Time of Angels.* **New York: Hyperion, 1995.**
Hannah, a young Jewish girl in 1918 Boston, has visions of angels soaring in the sky, sweeping over the city's rooftops and alleys and spires. She is visited by a girl with violet eyes, who guides and protects her and then disappears. Fleeing a deadly flu epidemic, Hannah finds herself in a place utterly different from Boston, where she encounters a stranger who nurses her back to health and helps her gain new perspectives on her life. Ages 12 and up.

Lewis, C. S. *The Lion, the Witch, and the Wardrobe.* **New York: Macmillan, 1950.**
In the first of the classic Chronicles of Narnia series, four young British children are transported to Narnia, where they engage in the Narnians' struggles against the powers of evil. Aslan, the golden lion, is their champion and savior. Aslan is strongly reminiscent of Christ, but the stories are not laden with a specifically Christian message. Ages 7 and up.

Lowry, Lois. *The Giver.* **New York: Bantam Doubleday Dell, 1993.**
The world in which Jonas lives denies a spiritual dimension in life. It is also devoid of color, of emotion, of imagination, of sexuality, of choice. When Jonas is chosen as the Receiver of Memories and begins to experience these dimensions of life, he reaches a spiritual crisis and must make a radical, life-changing decision. A Newbery Award winner. Ages 10–12.

Paulsen, Gary. *The Island.* **New York: Orchard, 1988.**
Wil Neuton discovers an island in a lake near his home and is drawn to return to the island again and again. There, for the first time, he observes the natural world closely, discovering hidden truths about nature, about life, and about his connection to other living things. He begins to draw what he sees, to write about it, to dance with it, to meditate. Wil is not immune to violence on the island, however, nor is his experience immune to media exploitation. Ages 12 and up.

Anthologies

Hamilton, Virginia. *In the Beginning: Creation Stories from Around the World.* **Barry Moser, illus. San Diego: Harcourt Brace, 1988.**
In these creation myths, Hamilton captures the commonalities and differences in humankind's desire to understand the origin and workings of

the universe. At the end of the book, she provides a brief analysis of types of creation myths, which is an excellent springboard for comparison and discussion. Ages 9 and up.

MacDonald, Margaret Read. *Peace Tales: World Folktales to Talk About.* **Atlanta: August House, 1992.**
MacDonald has collected folktales and proverbs about peace from many lands. She avoids "facile stories suggesting that we all simply join hands and love each other," choosing instead stories that illustrate what leads to war as well as to peace, emphasizing that peace is a choice and not always an easy one. While sometimes a story is better "left to settle in the listener's thoughts on its own," she has chosen stories that also lend themselves to discussion. Ages 8 and up.

REFERENCES

Bakhtin, M. M. (1981). *The dialogic imagination.* (Emerson, C., and Holquist, M., Trans.). Austin: University of Texas Press.

Berryman, J. (1991). *Godly play: An imaginative approach to religious education.* Minneapolis, MN: Augsburg.

———. (2002). *The complete guide to godly play: An imaginative method for presenting scripture stories to children.* Vol. 2. Denver: Living the Good News.

Bruner, J. (1986). *Actual minds, possible worlds.* Cambridge, MA: Harvard University Press.

Daniels, H. (1994). *Literature circles: Voice and choice in the student-centered classroom.* York, ME: Stenhouse.

Harste, J., Short, K., & Burke, C. (1988). *Creating classrooms for authors: The reading-writing connection.* Portsmouth, NH: Heinemann.

Hart, T. (2003). *The secret spiritual world of children.* Makawao, HI: Inner Ocean.

Hay, D., with R. Nye. (1998). *The spirit of the child.* London: Fount.

Moore, M. E. (1998). *Teaching from the heart.* Harrisburg, PA: Trinity Press International.

Rosen, H. (1986). The importance of story. *Language Arts, 63*(3), 226–237.

Rosenblatt, L. (1978). *The reader, the text, the poem.* Carbondale: Southern Illinois University Press.

Trousdale, A. M. (2001). Parallels, polarities, and intersections: Gender and religion in children's books. In S. Lehr (Ed.), *Beauty, brains, and brawn: The construction of gender in children's literature* (pp. 176–185). Portsmouth, NH: Heinemann.

5

✛

The Six Passages of Childhood: A Model for School-Based Rites of Passage

Rachael Kessler, with Laura Weaver

Two weeks before graduation, twenty-five seniors gather with their parents and teachers for a "senior honoring ceremony" to celebrate the gifts of each of these students—not just the few who have shown outstanding achievement in academics or athletics. This ceremony is a culminating moment in the Senior Passage program—a school-based rites-of-passage course designed to support one of the most vulnerable passages in the life cycle: the transition at the end of high school when childhood truly ends and the freedom and responsibility of adulthood loom, evoking excitement, confusion, and grief in students and their families.

A vase filled with a variety of long-stemmed flowers sits in the center of a softly lit room. The inner circle of chairs holds twenty-five students and the teachers who will address them. In the outer circle of chairs sit parents and other faculty members. After a welcome by the school principal, teachers walk one at a time to the center of the circle, select a unique flower from the vase, and stand before a surprised and curious student.

One teacher begins: "Scott, I have watched you grow this last year and become strong like the sturdy stalk of this giant iris. When you came into my class, I could tell that you were used to being one of the clowns. Yet, when it came time to share our stories, you took the first risk. You inspired all of us with the courage of your vulnerability. I want to honor you for the warmth you brought to each of us and the initiative and courage you've shown. I respect you as a leader and value you as a friend."

Scott beams. His father, behind him, looks stunned. This is his younger son—the cutup, the disappointment after the academic achiever who went before him, the one who has brought his father too many times to the disciplinary dean's office. After listening to one of the most respected teachers in the school celebrate the outstanding gifts of character this boy has demonstrated in his final year of high school, the father's face is soft, tears glistening. He places his hands on his son's broad shoulders. One squeeze tells the boy that his father has heard, that he sees him in a new light.

At the juncture between adolescence and adulthood—a time of anticipation, exhilaration, uncertainty, and fear—Scott discovered a chance to transform. In the dissolving of an adolescent identity before an adult identity emerges, many young people experience an opening to spirit. The "big" questions become urgent—questions of meaning and purpose, love and its shadows, integrity, and ultimate beginnings and endings. Without support, this year can be a time of loneliness and regression. Scott flourished in his final year of high school because this secular school had created a place for his soul. Senior Passages provided a forum where students were witnessed and honored by their peers and elders, given tools to navigate their transition, and guided by a curriculum that placed the students' usually unspoken questions and concerns at its center.[1]

Another vulnerable transition at the other end of the continuum of schooling is the initiation into kindergarten. After her son participated in a kindergarten rites-of-passage program, one mother noted the growth and change she saw in him:

> An extraordinary component of the Kindergarten Rites of Passage program is that it encourages communication and self-awareness through reflection. There are very few opportunities for children to reflect on the past, to look closely at the present, and then to communicate the sense of growth between the two. My son took great pride in realizing the social and emotional growth he has achieved over time: from a tentative experimenter with things new, to a bold and active do-er who now thrives in trying new things. A tremendous conversation erupted from this reflection. Why had he changed? To what does he attribute his growth? My son was then able to define the reason for his progression from tentative to bold, pinpointing his newfound idea of success as the key. In the past, success used to be found only in the winning outcome. Today, my son sees that success is also found in the trying, the effort, the process. (excerpted from parent feedback)

These stories illustrate the impact of school-based rites of passage (SBROP) on two of the six critical transition years in the life cycle of K–12 education. Each year that begins and ends a new level of schooling is a time of enormous change—for students, family, and faculty. While each transition has its unique developmental issues, there are also challenges and opportunities common to all of these years that reflect underlying patterns present in any major life shift.

THE NEED FOR RITES OF
PASSAGE ACROSS THE GRADE LEVELS

Anxiety, confusion, and regression, as well as relief, excitement, and new possibilities for transformation, are common for human beings when biology, culture, or social roles demand a developmental leap forward. On the threshold of the unknown, students must say good-bye not only to relationships with others but also to a childhood self. Apprehension and angst are normal during these profound changes. Mood swings are common among both the student and parents experiencing the shock of letting go of the past and the known. Family relationships may become volatile at this time—familiar patterns and parent–child roles often shift, bringing much confusion in their wake. As the child struggles with a new identity, parents are challenged to let go of one way of parenting and discover new ways to be responsible, caring guides for this young person who is ready for more (but not full) responsibility and freedom.

Faculty who teach students in transition often feel undermined by the students' restlessness, loss of interest in school, or general sense of upheaval. Teachers of fifth-grade students worry about the once sweet children who now lord their power over the younger children on the playground. Among high school seniors, even the most disciplined students may lose their capacity for focus. "Senioritis" jeopardizes the quality of learning and the once harmonious climate between student and teacher. These kinds of experiences are common when confidence is shaken as students stand on the brink of the unknown. I believe that the lack of support for transitions and the absence of initiation experiences may directly impact the high dropout rates we are seeing nationally in first-year students in both high school and college.

A growing body of research now acknowledges the challenges of the transition years. Researchers see that "there is consistent student achievement loss associated with the transition from self-contained elementary schools to intermediate-level schools" (Alspaugh & Harting, 1995). In our high schools, "29 of 51 states see their greatest 'leakage' in the education pipeline during the ninth grade" (EPE Research Center, 2006). According to the June 2010 report "Diplomas Count" by the EPE

Research Center, nationally, 1.3 million students will not graduate. That amounts to a loss of 7,200 students from the U.S. graduation pipeline every school day, or one student every 25 seconds (EPE Research Center, 2010). Increasingly, researchers suggest that the stress of unsupported transitions contributes to risky behavior in youth.[2] Taken together, these studies communicate the critical need for rites of passage and transition support expressed in our young people.

PROMOTING RESILIENCE, AWAKENING POSSIBILITY

I have primarily explored the risks associated with critical transition times in the life cycle of schooling. There are also gifts that arise during these turning points that can be nurtured or amplified with caring, thoughtfully structured support. Along with turmoil, transitions elicit an exhilarating awakening in young people. In the previous kindergarten parent's observations, we see the awakening to self-awareness that can happen during that vulnerable transition.

Even as early as fifth grade, students begin to glimpse the possibility of larger purpose and deeper meaning in life. They begin to explore their personal mysteries:

- Who am I?
- Do I have a purpose?
- Is there a God?
- How can people who love you hurt you? Why?
- What happens after you die?
- Why is it so hard to forgive?
- Will the Earth survive for my children and grandchildren?
- How come people hate others—black, white, Hispanic?
- Why is the spring so full?
- What makes some people so much more giving and loving than others?

Supported by a community of peers and caring elders during their transitions, students of all ages can develop a capacity for calm and confidence, openness to and compassion for the "Other," wonder and delight about exploring new relationships and beginning a new phase of schooling and personal identity. When students are given tools and experiences for constructively moving through major identity shifts, they are sustained not only in those particular moments of change but for each subsequent transition as well. Guided and validated by caring and creative adults, young people can make decisions that truly serve their own growth and the health of the community. Offered these opportunities in school, students also become more engaged and motivated to learn.

Recognizing the need to support young people through the challenges of transition, I have worked with colleagues across the country to develop structures and experiences that allow students' gifts to be revealed and celebrated during this time. We have turned for guidance to the ancient frameworks of rites of passage provided to us by cultures around the world.

RITES OF PASSAGE FOR ADOLESCENTS:
THE NEED AND OPPORTUNITY

Traditional and indigenous cultures teach us that adolescence is a particularly important stage in the spiritual life cycle. Virtually every preindustrial culture provided rites of initiation that helped their youths navigate the dangerous waters between childhood and adulthood. Many experts believe that the need for initiation is an essential one for growing to maturity and is hard-wired into adolescence (Mahdi, Christopher, & Meade, 1996; Mahdi, Foster, & Little, 1987).

Without constructive rites of passage provided by adults, teenagers in our communities create their own badges of adulthood—from the relatively benign driver's licenses, proms, and graduation ceremonies to the more dangerous extremes of binge drinking, first baby, first jail sentence, or even first murder. "If the fires that innately burn inside youths are not intentionally and lovingly added to the hearth of community," says poet Michael Meade, "they will burn down the structures of culture, just to feel the warmth" (1993, p. 19). These same adolescent fires can be cultivated and tended to in ways that revitalize the community, rather than destroy it.

While some American teenagers are blessed with meaningful confirmations—bar and bat mitzvahs in the Jewish community, *quinceañera* ceremonies in the Mexican community, initiation journeys offered by Buddhist or African American communities, fee-for-service wilderness programs based in a rites-of-passage model, and so on—most of our youths today have no opportunity to be guided by responsible adults through the loneliness, confusion, and wonder of the adolescent journey. Without these critical initiations, young people and their communities are diminished. "Because of the unhappy loss of this kind of initiatory experience, the modern world suffers a kind of spiritual poverty and a lack of community," says Malidoma Some (1994). "Young people are feared for their wild and dangerous energy, which is really an unending longing for initiation" (p. 68). SBROP programs can address this need for the many students who would never receive such guidance and challenge elsewhere. They offer young people a place to authentically express the challenges and transformative power that lies within their adolescent passage.

RITES OF PASSAGE FOR ADOLESCENTS: AN ANCIENT MODEL

Ancient and indigenous wisdom has provided critical grounding, concepts, and metaphors to build upon: elders take responsibility for creating a carefully sequenced experience that temporarily removes initiates from ordinary life and provides an opportunity for adolescents to be challenged and stretched to let go of childish ways and learn new skills and attitudes for being a more responsible adult. The last phase of the initiation involves some kind of ceremonial acknowledgment by the adult community that the young person has graduated into his or her new role. In such cultures, this welcoming of the new adults reflects a belief that rites of passage not only support the initiates but also revitalize the adult community as they benefit from the gifts these new members bring.

In 1909, anthropologist Arnold van Gennep (2004), the first to use the term "rite of passage," discovered that throughout the world there were commonly three phases associated with adolescent initiation experiences: severance, threshold, and reincorporation.[3] The following summary of these phases blends ancient principles and modern thinking that were integrated into my own understanding when first writing about rites of passage in my book *The Soul of Education.*

Phase 1, *severance* (separation and/or cutting away), provides a real or symbolic separation from what is known, familiar, and secure. Initiates are encouraged to experience and express loss as part of this separation, to say good-bye, and to understand that, in loss, they make room for something new to come in. Initiates are also invited to cut away or let go of aspects of the self that no longer serve and to recognize the need to prune away qualities, habits, or old ways of relating that may have been useful in the last stage of life but would hold them back from growing into the next.

Phase 2, the *threshold* or liminal phase, represents the in-between time in which the old identity has been shattered or dissolved, leading to a seemingly interminable period of nothingness, a lack of identity, before the new self begins to form. During this stage, a person can feel disoriented, lost, and confused. The roots of the word *confusion* mean "to pour together," because contradictory aspects of the old and new may intermingle.

Phase 3, *reincorporation*, or reintegration, invites initiates to reenter their worldly lives and communities, bringing the gifts of their visions and newly emerging identities. This may also involve offering a physical gift to others in the community. Elders create rituals that honor, witness, and incorporate the initiates into the community of adults. And in contemporary models that utilize retreats that evoke a dramatic experience of passage, reentry also prepares youths for the abrupt and often painfully dissonant experience of coming back into ordinary life.[4]

THE SIX PASSAGES OF CHILDHOOD

Before we provide one model of an SBROP that adapts these ancient and modern principles into a phased approach to supporting transitions in school, we will look at the unique issues, challenges, and opportunities associated with each of the six passages of youth. Like the ancient models, we initially began our work with SBROP by developing a curriculum for the passage from adolescence into adulthood. But over the last decade, we have extended this model to support each of the six passages of childhood. In discussing the issues that arise with each developmental transition, we have used the names from the PassageWorks Institute curriculum that specifically address those transitions and have included the voices of teachers, students, and parents who have been impacted by this particular model of SBROP-VIII.

I. First Steps into Elementary School: The Passage into Kindergarten

In kindergarten, students leave behind their first phase of childhood and begin the cognitive, social, emotional, and spiritual journey of school life.[5] Some children are entering school for the first time after being at home with parents or another caretaker, while others have spent time in preschool settings or neighborhood playgroups. Whatever their prior experience, when students enter kindergarten, they must rely on themselves, their peers, and their teachers to keep them safe and provide nurturing support at school. New experiences with academic learning stretch kindergartners' creative and critical thinking capacities as they connect new concepts to prior knowledge and express ideas and questions. This transition benefits from a strong parent component, and SBROP can assist kindergartners and their parents to constructively navigate newly emerging independence.

A teacher in a small, rural, primarily low-income school in Missouri writes about her SBROP: "Whether you came to school from government-funded housing projects or the subdivisions of modern homes with fenced yards, when soul enters the classroom, every heart has equal value." Another teacher notes that, after implementing an SBROP, "students are more connected to one another and more confident as individuals, have fewer arguments, are adept at resolving conflicts, working in pairs and groups, and have a good basis for knowing and discussing their feelings."

II. Healthy Transitions out of Elementary School: The Fifth- or Sixth-Grade Passage

Students of this age develop increased self-awareness, become more aware of peer relationships and gender differences, and begin to individuate from their parents and from adults in general. They wonder and worry about how they will deal with the new expectations, routines, responsibilities, and relationships of middle school. In addition to this movement from the known to the unknown, students are rapidly changing physically and physiologically as puberty becomes central to their life experience. Preparing students for this passage involves sharing tools that will help them cope and thrive. By strengthening their sense of who they are and identifying what they personally value, students develop resources to make good choices, say good-bye to what they are leaving behind, become open to the new, and ride the storms of puberty.

"PassageWorks has strengthened our connections to one another while adding a whole new depth to our community," writes one teacher. Another teacher in a public focus school where students stayed with their class and teacher for the entire elementary school experience comments: "I've worked with most of these students for five years now. I thought I knew them so well. But doing PassageWorks with them in their final year, I have come to know them at an entirely new level. As a man and a teacher, this has been a profound experience for me—to come so close to these young people, to be trusted with their hearts, and inspired by their wisdom."

III. Entering the Culture of Middle School: The Sixth- or Seventh-Grade Transition

As students leave the smaller, more intimate community of elementary schools and enter the larger world of middle school, they are called to develop increased capacities for maturity, responsibility, and self-management. SBROP can support these incoming middle school students to strengthen their individual identities, while fostering meaningful new relationships across social divides. By promoting a culture of kindness and emotional and social competence, schools can mitigate the slide into incivility, insecurity, and peer cruelty common to the middle school years.

A seventh-grade teacher in a Jewish day school in Florida writes: "As the weeks progress, so do the activities. We move into dyads and circles, and the topics become deeper. They reflect the children's greatest hopes and fears. Students frequently note that we all share the same things. Students talk to people that they may not usually talk to, and a level of trust has been established."

After his first year of implementing PassageWorks, a sixth-grade teacher wrote: "I have never had kids who treated each other with such kindness. One girl who conveyed in early Councils that she had always been excluded was actually taken under the wings of a group of the 'popular' girls who were determined to protect her and give her an entirely different experience." This kind of behavior in the classroom builds trust and belonging among students, supports a new ground for relationships, and cultivates confidence and resilience.

IV. Completing Middle School: The Eighth- or Ninth-Grade Transition

Students at this age live on a razor's edge between early and late adolescence. As reflected in national dropout statistics, the transition between middle school and high school is one of the most vulnerable times in a student's career, and we lose far too many students to this transition. SBROP programs can mitigate this trend by preparing middle school students for the new environments they will encounter in high school, supporting them in saying good-bye to relationships that aren't working or may no longer be available, cultivating their ability to deal with stress and meet increased academic demands, and providing opportunities for them to adjust to larger, more diverse school populations.

At a time when youths are becoming increasingly aware of differences, they are often unsure how to appreciate or even tolerate these aspects of other students' identities. End-of-middle-school programs can help students understand that differences don't have to be feared and, to the contrary, can add vibrancy and depth to a community in a way that is deeply satisfying.

Finally, SBROP can moderate the tendency for students to "check out" and disengage from school, supporting students to make essential connections between academic content and their personal lives. "Passage-Works allows me to know my students as individual human beings with fears, insecurities, hopes, and dreams," writes an eighth-grade language arts teacher. "In the classroom I can challenge them more, push them further, and move them through the content more easily because I know them and they feel safe with me. They trust me and try harder because they know that I care about them. The best parts of PassageWorks are the moments when I am surprised by the depth of thought, maturity, and selflessness demonstrated in these weekly lessons that I don't always see on a day to day basis."

V. Journey into High School

The transition to high school is fraught with complexity. This phase of adolescence often brings mood swings, antiauthoritarianism, cynicism, divisive clique formation, and intense emotions. Feelings of loneliness and isolation are common as friendships shift, transform, and fall away. Students of this age are caught in a paradox: they seek to know and assert themselves in more depth and uniqueness, while wanting and needing to belong and fit in. And because students at this age frequently lack the strong sense of self required to stand up to a variety of pressures, they are more vulnerable to the allure of risky and self-destructive behaviors.

As freshmen and sophomores differentiate from parents and teachers, they may assume the appearance and posture of young adulthood, though inside they are often emotionally young and extremely vulnerable. A sophomore teacher notes, "These students are a lot younger than they look." Because of their earnest need to look mature, some are reluctant to engage in play, movement, or other creative expression they fear might make them look childish.

At the same time, high school students often begin their quest for deeper meaning and purpose, and they experience a desire to take on more personal and social responsibility. Students come to know their personal passions and long for a way to express these in the world, making this a ripe time for including activities that connect the inner life with the outer world. This is also a time when students yearn for guidance from mature adults and mentors and for safe environments where they can take risks, drop their social masks, and discover and reveal glimpses of their authentic selves.

An advisory teacher speaks to the beauty of these moments she has had with her students: "The whole class, every single student, was really present. They are beginning to really care about each other, even with their differences. They are respecting each other. A group of twenty-five students from such different social groups sitting together at 8:20 in the morning really being present and listening to each other—that is powerful."

VI. Senior Passages

As students prepare to move into college or the world at large, they must cope with the pressure of crucial decisions and anticipate the emotional shock of leaving behind nurturing relationships that have supported them for their entire life of K–12 schooling—parents, siblings, teachers, and friends. On the threshold of the unknown, seniors must let go of relationships not only with others but also with a childhood self and an adolescent identity that will no longer serve them in the adult life that awaits them. Learning about grief, closure, and healthy good-byes is vital to entering their next phase with resilience and openness.

Seniors often show a longing for wholeness and authenticity—they are fascinated by honest explorations of the hidden realms of consciousness and the unconscious. And, in contrast with earlier adolescence, seniors are often ready to let go of pretense and reclaim the playfulness and creativity of childhood. To thrive, seniors must learn to cope with stress and to make decisions that reflect their authentic values, priorities, and goals.

"This class has provided me with an environment that allows me to clear my head, slow down, and make healthy choices for me," wrote one student about Senior Passages. "It makes me realize just how unique each individual's experience is, and the importance of listening. A senior in high school must make colossal decisions whether he or she is ready or not. The more people can be honest about and aware of their own needs when making these decisions, the healthier the decisions will be."

After experiencing the impact of an SBROP on her family, a mother commented: "We have always been such a tight family. But we just didn't know how to do this good-bye thing. I don't know what we would have done without the course. It really helped us see that we could let go and still remain loving. And for my daughter, the most amazing thing was the way she got so close to students she had judged so harshly those first weeks of the course. She started college with such an open mind, and so much more resilience."

VII. A Seventh Passage: Newcomer Students

In the midst of a life-altering transition, recently immigrated students—or newcomers—often enter the U.S. school system filled with grief, intense yearning for their homeland, confusion about the multiple identities and alliances they are now juggling, and excitement about new opportunities and potentials. Many newcomer students arrive after having experienced significant traumas—from geographic dislocation and family breakups to physical duress, harassment, and violence. And because much of immigration is driven by an economic imperative, adolescent immigrants often feel the dual pressure of performing in school while holding down one or more jobs to help support the family.

When newcomer students are offered the opportunity to honor the people, lands, cultures, and personal identities they have left behind and to reclaim and integrate aspects of their past, they become empowered to move forward with strength and confidence. As one teacher of newcomers wrote about her SBROP: "Students are able to let down their academic guards and assume their authentic personalities. With Transitions

Programs in place, students are more likely to embrace learning and language acquisition for themselves."

SBROP: ONE MODEL THAT
SUPPORTS EACH OF THE K–12 TRANSITIONS

In *The Soul of Education,* I mapped a set of spiritual yearnings called the "seven gateways," based on what students described about their experiences, whether or not they have a religious or spiritual tradition. Each of the seven gateways to the inner life of students articulates a different way young people experience deep connection with themselves, others, and the world. Together, these gateways offer both a language and a framework, providing useful guidance about how to structure rites-of-passage work to meet the needs, yearnings, and passions of young people (see figure 5.1). The seventh gateway, Initiation, describes the need for young people to have adults in their lives who can provide a conscious, deliberate and structured process for initiating them into the next phase of their development" (Kessler, 2000).

Building on the principles and practices that are common to initiation in many cultures, I defined a rite of passage as a *structured* process, *guided by adults,* in which young people are:

- helped to become *conscious about the irrevocable transition* they're in,
- *given tools* for making transitions and separations,
- *initiated* into the new *capacities* required for their next step, and
- *acknowledged* by the community of adults, as well as their peers, for their courage and strength in taking that step.

This definition was originally derived from work with adolescents and formed the basis of the Senior Passage curriculum (see Kessler, 2006).

deep connection: connecting to self, others, nature, a higher power or faith tradition

silence: inviting reflection, fertile chaos, rest, stillness, prayer or contemplation

meaning and purpose: exploring existential questions, values and goals, service

joy: creating opportunities for play, celebration, gratitude, beauty, grace, love

creativity: encouraging artistic expression, new ideas, visions, and discoveries

transcendence: acknowledging the yearning to stretch beyond perceived limits

initiation: guiding and honoring youth through their transitions

Figure 5.1.   The Seven Gateways

Since the formation of the PassageWorks Institute in 2001,[6] our school-based approach to rites of passage evolved to provide professional development for teachers and a transition curriculum specific to each transition year. We adapted the Senior Passage model to develop the tools, frameworks, and experiences that appropriately support younger children as they enter and leave each phase in the life cycle of schooling.

Here, I want to describe how we have built on and adapted the traditional three-phase rites-of-passage model to serve this need for transition support in each of the six passages in schools. The following outline underlies each of our curricula and describes the themes of each phase and the flow from one phase to another. With appropriate adaptations to developmental needs and capacities, these phases inform our PassageWorks programs at each grade level.

Phase 1: Building Community and Preparing for the Journey

PassageWorks often begins with the metaphor of the *journey* and describes this phase as "building the boat" that will keep us safe as we leave the shore of what has been familiar and comfortable to enter a new phase of our lives and our identities. Students build community with one another, begin to risk the waters of self-knowledge, and connect to people whom they have previously judged as too different from themselves.

Phase 2: Severance or Letting Go

In the words of William Bridges (1980):

> Transition does not require that you reject or deny the importance of your old life, just that you let go of it. Far from rejecting it, you are likely to do better with the ending if you honor the old life for all that it did for you. It got you this far. It brought you everything you have. But now, although it may be some time before you are comfortable actually doing so, it is time for you to let go of it. (p. 16)[7]

Like Bridges, I have seen throughout my work with youths in transition that it is easier to let go of a phase of life or aspect of our identity if we first give it attention and honor. In this phase, our programs provide time for students to look back at childhood before we invite them to release their childish ways and identities. They reflect on who they were in the past, sift and sort what they cherished about their childhood, and decide what no longer serves them as they go forward. We make the distinction between the "childish"—habits and beliefs that students have outgrown—and "childlike" qualities such as playfulness, creativity, and wonder that may need to be reclaimed after a period of cynicism or trying to act mature. This phase allows students to move on more consciously and with greater authenticity to the responsibilities and decisions that lie just beyond their current stage of schooling and psychosocial development.

Phase 3: Threshold or Stretching

In this phase, students are encouraged to stretch inwardly and outwardly. They name their personal mysteries; explore larger issues of personal and social responsibility in light of social and global conditions; look forward to the future; set goals that emerge from their authentic values, priorities, and dreams; and identify inner and outer obstacles to and resources for meeting those goals and realizing their dreams.

Phase 4: Reintegration and Completion

This phase fosters consciousness about negative patterns of endings and offers a model for saying good-bye in ways that leave us whole. We live in a culture that tends to avoid good-byes, which often remind us of the "big good-bye"—death. Small losses remind us of big losses. And because adults in this culture have had little support or education in dealing with the grief dimension of closure, they often feel awkward about good-byes. Consequently, students have seen few models for constructive closure. Conscious closure, on the other hand, brings a sense of completion. While there may still be feelings of loss or sadness, the student also feels the fullness and satisfaction of having been part of meaningful relationships. Then, when the time is right, these young people will be able to approach a new situation or relationship with an open heart and mind.

CEREMONIES TO ENHANCE RITES OF PASSAGE

Our curricula often culminate in a ceremony involving parents, faculty, and students, in which the community of elders acknowledge each student personally for his or her growth to new levels of maturity. The faculty version of that ceremony was described in the opening story of this chapter. The following describes our parent model.

Parents are engaged early in the year through lessons from the curriculum in which students are encouraged to interview their parents, guardians, or mentors about their heritage, the origin of their name, early impressions of their child, and so forth. Beyond this, teachers host two evenings for parents in which they follow outlines that define a process for both introduction and closure.

The first is for parents only and provides information and experiential practice with the new tools their children are experiencing during the weekly PassageWorks hour. After a brief introduction, a playful focusing activity, and a dyad for practicing deep listening and authentic speaking, parents are led in a sharing circle or council in which they can share with the group (if they choose) what's working well and what's challenging about parenting their child, who is starting or leaving elementary school, entering middle school or high school, or making the leap to leave school and, often, home behind for college, work, or the military. Parents are delighted to have a forum to express these feelings and learn from each other's wisdom.

The second evening, which comes at the end of the semester, is the ceremony that marks the completion of one stage and the student's passage into the next step of development. During the culminating ceremony, we hold a Witness Council. Students, witnessed by parents, sit in an inside circle with their teacher and speak about how they feel about taking this next step. After the students finish sharing, a few parents are asked to speak about what they just witnessed. From fifth-grade parents, we often hear statements like: "I can't believe these kids are so articulate" or "I can't believe that my son is ready—he's really ready. He couldn't sleep at the beginning of fifth grade."

Two parents of seniors captured what so many parents feel at this moment: "I feel hope for the future for the first time," said one father jumping up to speak. "I'm a coach, I work with young people all the time, but I never get to hear their innermost thoughts. I can't believe how articulate and wise these kids are!" "I knew my son was dealing with these feelings, even though he's reluctant to tell us sometimes," said a mother. "But listening to the same feelings coming from so many students, it helps me understand and appreciate my own son so much better."

At this point in the ceremony, we ask the parents to close their eyes and remember a precious moment when their son or daughter was two or three years old, focusing intently on that image in their minds. Next they open their eyes and look at their son or daughter and then publicly, in front of the whole community, acknowledge the growth that they have seen.

> "You make me so proud," said one fifth grader's father to his son as the circles of students and parents looked on. "What I'm remembering is, you're two years old, maybe one and a half. You're in my arms and you're drawing on the condensation on the window, and I said, 'What are you making?' You said, 'I'm making an anaconda which is evaporating into a bird.'" The son and the whole group erupted into warm laughter as the father made big flapping gestures with his arms. "I could picture these little bits of water evaporating up into birds. You're so creative and so articulate, and you have such a beautiful heart."

In the senior–parent ceremonies, the tears flow from the mothers and often from the daughters, with many parents and students moved by the depth of feeling and healing as parents seize this rare opportunity to publicly honor their own child. When the seniors themselves are asked to speak about what it is like to witness this, they share the new respect they feel for adults as they witness their honesty, their caring, and the struggle to be a good parent and to let go.

In many of the fifth-grade ceremonies I have witnessed, tears flow from fathers and sons, as well. Fathers and sons embrace. And the eleven-year-olds, when asked to witness what they have just seen, make comments like, "It is so interesting to see adults become so emotional!" or "I have been with these friends for five years and I thought I really knew them, but I have learned so much more when I listen to the people who live with them twenty-four hours a day."

In one eighth-grade parent ceremony, I was most struck by a young girl who said, "I always thought my parents would think of me like I do when I think of the worst of me. But I was amazed today to see all the gifts they see in me and the continuity they see in who I really am ever since I was little." I learned that this girl went on to become a leader during her high school years.

Each time I have led or witnessed a parent-honoring ceremony at the different transitions, I have felt that these students have just been surrounded by the strongest shield of protection possible for this next phase of their journey. I believe that beginning a new school, a new phase of life, a new social group, or a new identity with the explicit knowledge that your parents love, respect, know, and believe in who you are brings a quality of resilience, a willingness to resist the lure of risk and to listen to and heed the emerging guidance of your authentic self.

There is much to be gained in the experience and learning that comes just from a journey with students and teachers in school through a rites-of-passage curriculum. But when we can truly heed the wisdom of reincorporation by including parents, guardians, and other key adult mentors in honoring the young as they take these courageous steps, we protect our children so much more fully, and we inspire hope, renewal, and a new kind of responsibility as elders in the adult community.

CONCLUSION

Change can happen at any time, but transition comes along when one chapter of your life is over and another is waiting in the wings to make its entrance. . . . You simply cannot imagine a new chapter, but the fact is that letting go of one chapter in your life initiates the transition that concludes by beginning another chapter. (Bridges, 1980, p. 91)

Passages—major transitions—come at many points in the life cycle. Puberty, high school and college graduations, marriage, parenthood, midlife, old age, and death are what usually come to mind. I have been called at various times in my life to work with all of these turning points; I have taught workshops on the initiation into mothering and on the midlife quest and have written about the marriage journey. I have navigated my own separation, divorce, and renewal, am undergoing a rite of passage through cancer, and am now in the midst of a personal initiation into elderhood. I have raised three sons to adulthood and supported the birth of two grandsons and the journey of two daughters-in-law who transitioned from cultures that are vastly different from that of our family.

The opportunity to work with SBROP felt like a divine calling when it came in the mid-1980s. Since then, I have watched parents, students, and faculty impacted by simple but transformative rites-of-passage experiences. Through the collaboration and wisdom of thousands of teachers, students, and colleagues throughout the country, an SBROP model has emerged that can serve students across the spectrum of grades and schools. This rich learning led me and a group of dedicated colleagues to found the PassageWorks Institute—an organization dedicated to supporting students through critical life transitions and to reigniting the passion for teaching and mentoring within faculty.

It is my greatest intention that all students have access to the deep wisdom and transformative experiences embedded in rites-of-passage models. I believe that such work will serve not only to transform the lives of individuals but also to support the birth of a sustainable global culture at a time when our planet so desperately needs the wisdom, fire, insight, and responsibility of awakened youth and of empowered elders.

NOTES

I am deeply grateful for the collaboration of Laura Weaver, my partner in curriculum writing and implementation, and in extending the school-based rites of passage model from a program for high school seniors to a set of programs that support each transition in the "six passages of childhood." While the narrative voice is usually singular because of my engagement for over twenty years in the development of the core model that is the foundation of this story, Laura's contribution has been vital to reaching the scope and refinement of this chapter.

1. The Mysteries Program and the Senior Passages program at the Crossroads School in Santa Monica, California, was originally created by Jack Zimmerman, then president of the Ojai Foundation, in partnership with Maureen Murdock and Ruthann Saphier. I am deeply grateful for their genius in framing a model that I was privileged to grow, with the input of many other colleagues over the years, into an approach to SBROP that could serve other transitions as well.

2. "Stressful events, such as school transition, different stages of acculturation, and problems at home, may make students more vulnerable to experiment with alcohol, tobacco, and other drugs" (Comprehensive School Reform Quality Center, 2005, p. 31).

3. Others have demonstrated that this universal model is derived primarily from initiation practices for boys. The work of Carol Gilligan has certainly sensitized us to the need to look at developmental models with an eye toward gender differences. I have given much thought to this complex task in regard to rites of passage, but it goes beyond the scope of this chapter.

4. It is a common pattern for schools that hold a senior retreat to save the retreat for the last week of school. Students may have a powerful experience, but then are left on their own with no support to integrate the experience and the shock of return. Similarly, wilderness rites of passage often provide no support for reincorporation once the student returns home.

5. "Just as the body of the child will not grow if it is not fed, and the mind will not grow if it is not stimulated, a child's inner life must be nourished to develop" (Kessler, 2000, p. x). By "inner life" or "spiritual development," PassageWorks refers to that essential aspect of human nature that yearns for deep connection, grapples with questions of awe and wonder, and seeks a sense of genuine self-expression.

6. The PassageWorks Institute was founded in 2001 by myself and my colleagues to nourish the inner life of students through school-based rites of passage programs. See www.passageworks.org for more information.

7. William Bridges, listed by the *Wall Street Journal* as one of the top ten executive development presenters in America, has specialized in writing about transitions.

REFERENCES

Aber, J. L., Allen, L., Feinman, J., Mitchell, C., & Seidman, E. (1994). The impact of school transitions in early adolescence on the self-system and social context of poor urban youth. *Child Development, 65*, 507–522.

Alspaugh, J. W., & Harting, R. O. (1995). Transition effects of school grade-level organization on student achievement. *Journal of Research and Development in Education, 28*(3), 145–149.

Bridges, W. (1980). *Transitions: Making sense of life's changes.* Cambridge, MA: Perseus Books.

Comprehensive School Reform Quality Center. (2005). *Works in progress: A report on middle and high school improvement programs.* Washington, DC: Comprehensive School Reform Quality Center American Institutes for Research.

Crawford, A. M., Pentz, M. A., Chou, C. O., Li, C., & Dwyer, J. H. (2003). Parallel developmental trajectories of sensation seeking and regular substance use in adolescents. *Psychology of Addictive Behaviors, 17*(3), 179–192.

EPE Research Center. (2006). Diplomas count: An essential guide to graduation rates and policies. *Education Week.* Retrieved from www.edweek.org/ew/toc/2006/06/22/index.html.

EPE Research Center. (2010). Diplomas count: Graduation by the numbers. *Education Week*. Retrieved from www.edweek.org/ew/toc/2010/06/10/index.html.

Kessler, R. (2000). *The soul of education: Helping students find connection, compassion, and character at school*. Alexandria, VA: Association for Supervision and Curriculum Development.

———. (2006). The Senior Passage course. In Elias, M., & H. Arnold (Eds.), *The educator's guide to emotional intelligence and academic achievement* 247–258. Thousand Oaks, CA: Corwin Press.

Mahdi, L. C., Christopher, N. G., & Meade, M. (Eds.). (1996). *Crossroads: The quest for contemporary rites of passage*. Chicago: Open Court Press.

Mahdi, L. C., Foster, S., & Little, M. (Eds.). (1987). *Betwixt and between: Patterns of masculine and feminine initiation*. La Salle, IL: Open Court Press.

6

✛

Paying Attention to the Whole Self

Peter Perkins

Growing up on the family farm in southern Wisconsin had me driving tractors at nine years old, plowing eighty-acre fields, tightening barbed wire to hold the Hereford cows in the pasture, racing with my brothers to fill the haymow before a rainstorm, and feeding cattle every morning and afternoon. It was the life I knew, and I liked it.

Attending school in the nearby city introduced me to peers who did not do what I did every day. I had often wondered what city kids did after school, on weekends, or on vacations. At around thirteen years old, I discovered that they were not working as much as I was. I soon recognized there was another way to be a kid, unlike what was common among my country friends. I began to spend occasional time in town, and, by the time I was driving to high school, I longed to spend much more time with the kids in town.

This chapter explores how growing up can be either a flat, anxious, and frustrating experience or a challenging and fulfilling time—how weaving youthful experiences with one's source of inner strength can produce a deep well of hope, patience, and integrity from which to draw throughout life. A youth's developmental journey follows a unique blend of emotional textures, purposeful directions, aimlessness, and fun, reflecting diverse human dimensions that make up our complete selves. Each of these dimensions provides certain capacities and can inform us as we befriend and support youths as they develop and grow.

Working on the farm six days a week, Sunday seemed like simply getting a day off. I eventually came to realize that Sunday was about taking the time to breathe in more of who I might be in the world. I could stop, listen, relax, see friends, try something different, watch football with my dad, go to church, and enjoy a family feast.

TO SURVIVE OR TO THRIVE?

After leaving the farm, I traveled around the United States for four years. It was a journey of happenstance; I went from one adventure to another. I got to Aspen, Colorado, from Las Vegas only because one day the wind was blowing northeast. My buddy, Gos, and I were in search of work and had only enough gas money to get to Denver or Los Angeles, so the extra help of the wind propelled my VW microbus north to the Rockies.

After a few months of working as a maid and learning to ski, I noticed that a group of people were organizing the first crisis-counseling center in Pitkin County, Colorado. I had spied an article in the *Aspen Times* seeking volunteers and decided to try it. My true motive at first was to meet some locals and get away from the transient life of that old gold-mining town turned high-mountain ski resort. Dave was one of the first people who befriended me among this group of hippies, ski bums, and local businesspeople gathered at that initial meeting in the snowy spring of 1975. We talked about a new idea called "wellness and well-being." Dave told me about the Aspen Institute, wellness programs, and his work as spiritual wellness adviser to folk musician John Denver. Dave and I eventually worked together as deputy sheriffs in the Pitkin County jailhouse researching wellness and the effects of nutrition on criminal behavior.

At nineteen years old, I had my first "holistic" wellness experience with his help. Training in the Art of Loving began on a Friday evening in 1972 at an isolated monastery in the mountains of Old Snowmass. I was the youngest of eighteen other unsuspecting adults gathered for this forty-hour intensive retreat into our deeper selves. I delved into aspects of myself I never had a name for or even knew were part of me. My Catholic upbringing had familiarized me with rituals, which grounded me for some of this, but the psychological, emotional, and even physical work made me vulnerable, yet open and honest, to seeing my own life patterns, fears, and hopes. The experience was safe enough to accept this challenge of self-exploration. What I learned about myself and everyone else that weekend planted a persistent question in my mind. This query has led me from being a dirt farmer who had missed spring planting for the first time that year, through my careers of crisis and substance-abuse counseling and prevention work, and on to education.

The persistent question looks mostly like this: If holistic wellness is about caring for the whole person, and if as human beings we are of many dimensions which help us to survive, to be healthy, and potentially to thrive, then what are these essential dimensions, and shouldn't everyone—parents and friends of youths, as well as professional teachers, counselors, and service providers—know how to tap into them?

Today, I reflect on more than twenty-five years of crisis and drug counseling with adolescents and their families and can see that I was doing pretty well, known as an effective substance-abuse counselor in Vermont. Throughout those years, as my professional observations unfolded, I returned to that persistent question, a question that academics and practitioners are still struggling with: How does holistic wellness makes sense within the traditional fields of sociology, psychology, and education?

As a practitioner in the early days of substance-abuse treatment and prevention, I delved deeper into the spiritual question through a series of conferences organized with colleagues (see Perkins & Pransky, 1994). With over a hundred others, we explored the meaning of holistic, heart-based, and spiritual dimensions of life and considered how to include this definition in our work as educators and prevention practitioners with youths and adults. During this time, I decided to further study holistic development and apply my experiences to my work with youth and families. I enrolled in graduate school, finding there was tremendous interest in this question of holism and not very much written about it or practiced in the field of human services or public education. I sadly discovered that this was an idea whose time had apparently not yet come.

WELLNESS: PAYING ATTENTION TO THE WHOLE SELF

Most mechanistic responses to the human condition have led us down paths of parenting, education, and human services that treat people as individual parts that can be fixed or changed. A drug problem calls for a drug counselor; depression, a therapist, psychiatrist, or better therapeutic drugs; failing grades, a learning plan. We have worked hard to improve the lives of young people through an array of well-intentioned programs, interventions, creative initiatives, and community collaborations. However, rarely have we designed our work with the whole system in mind. Rarely have we assessed and drawn on the strengths of people in adverse circumstances or sought the deeper causes of the problems.

Over the past several years, attempts have been made to expand from the classic narrow approach to a more open, holistic system of care and encouragement that seeks to intervene with the whole and complex nature of the human condition. A drug problem, depression, or boredom is *not* an isolated event. These conditions exist because of societal, familial, and individual behaviors, norms, and attitudes. A holistic approach draws upon all the dimensions of the individual, the family, and the community so youths can thrive, not merely survive. An isolated intervention, while useful in the short term, becomes more valuable when it occurs in the whole context of a person's life. That person goes home to a family, lives in an environment, and is part of a personal history.

This "new" holistic way draws upon ancient thinking and practices such as the science of yoga, which seeks unity of mind, body, and soul. Native American teachings look to the medicine wheel for guidance to life by integrating the four directions of the mental, physical, emotional, and spiritual realms. Early philosophy and psychology yielded Carl Jung (1933), who wrote about a reawakening and rethinking of spirituality, along with William James (1952), who wrote about the "constituents of the self," which included the mental, material, and spiritual, all being guided by human volition. Some in the behaviorist tradition and the field of cognitive psychology wrote about the interplay among thoughts, feelings, and behaviors. So, with this limited research based on a more holistic view, I began my search for an inclusive model of human development, hoping to find a description of humanity that would give greater hope to my work with youths.

Holistic thinking about what it means to be a teenager was emerging more and more in the 1990s (see Perkins, 1991). Research on resiliency (Hendersen, 2007) has highlighted how youths buried in traumatic life experiences still have the ability to move beyond that and develop relatively healthy lives. Research on asset development suggested that there is a core of traits and behaviors that predispose a person to a reasonably healthy lifestyle (Bensen, 1997). A willingness to look at what is and is not making a difference with youths in schools, families, and counseling centers became evident in the field of human services—popularized with research-based programs. Funders began to ask the hard question of providers: How did we know that what we were doing made a difference? And they began requiring program choices to be science based to be funded.

The behaviorist approach, with proof of success determined primarily by observable behavior change, comes with a cost. Does it result in deep change or simply a shift in less risky behaviors? If the latter, what else is required for deep change? What does this deeper and more sustainable change, which may well include behavior, really look like? Take, for example, a sixteen-year-old who has stopped using marijuana, but who still lives with the stress of his alcoholic parent. Perhaps he developed inner skills and attitudes that have strengthened him to cope with each moment. He now smokes less pot, and perhaps has begun to feel that life has options. Maybe the marijuana use was an accessible coping mechanism and not the ultimate behavior that would determine whether or not this person would grow to be healthy and happy.

In the 1980s and 1990s, I helped adolescents shift from drug-taking and alcohol-drinking behaviors. Was this success? Maybe it was, but only to a degree, as few of these kids went on to thrive and realize their full potential. Did they function pretty well in their communities? Many did. But several fell back to similar or even new self-destructive behaviors. What I found most useful during my years of counseling youths was recognizing their individuality. In education, this individual assessment provides the basis for differentiating each student's learning process. In each youth I counseled, was his or her success in life held by internal capacities each possessed but didn't necessarily access? Ultimately, my work shifted from simply changing a drug-use behavior to helping youths find that deeper self to guide them through challenges and toward healthy decision making and happiness in life.

Parents, teachers, and counselors who have stepped back and discovered their own inner strengths and capacities come to mind as those who help our kids develop and become the best they can become. However, I found in my graduate research and my ongoing practice as a counselor and prevention practitioner that neither adults nor adolescents had consistently thought about, experienced, clarified, or drawn upon these capacities. In a life-skills-building workshop a father told me that he didn't have emotions—men don't do that. One woman told a group of parents that since she did not go to church, she did not think she had a spiritual self. Several parents blamed their children for being caught up in a material world with no other interests.

When asked, youths describe their spiritual selves, their inner source of strength. So perhaps the questions for all of us are: How can we adults help young people discover their wholeness and their wellness? Why don't we do it?

DIMENSIONS OF THE SELF

Through clinical observation and academic research on human development I developed the Five Dimensions of the Self (Perkins, 2003). The most obvious dimension was the Thinking Self. This can be seen daily in our interactions as parents and educators with adolescents, focusing on thoughts and ideas. Some say we create our reality through our thoughts (Pransky, 1998). What we think is what we experience.

Another dimension is the Feeling Self, acknowledged and explored in the counseling setting but not fully understood or explored through parenting or education. Emotional intelligence, as explored by Daniel Goleman (1995) and others, has come to be associated with deeper learning and can be seen as essential to a full expression of ourselves.

A third and profound dimension is the Material Self, which includes our physical aspect. It is essential to our survival, but often leads to excess, greed, and overconsumption. Youths can be susceptible to excessive material consumption; identity may become confused with outward appearance.

The Community Self is also a key dimension with adolescents and is equally essential for survival; we need others—human, animal, and plant—to survive and to go further and thrive as people. Youths tend to associate in groups, gangs, cliques, and teams, or resort to the other extreme, becoming loners. Adolescence is a time of beginning to distinguish who one is individually.

The dimension I found to be most consistently named or most obviously absent across the research was the Spiritual Self—that which describes the inner life, known uniquely by each person and accessed in a variety of ways, ranging from religion, walks in the woods, yoga, meditation, dance, and art to simple relaxation and thoughtful dialogue. Sometimes this is referred to as the deeper, heart-centered place in all of us that creates a well of inner strength upon which to draw in hard times and celebrate in good times. This is the dimension of our common human experience that has many interpretations. It is most often separated from the whole self and not included in the education of children or the human services that are provided them. Kids want to know themselves on a deeper level, especially as they progress through adolescence.

HOPE IN DIALOGUE

When given the opportunity, teens will go deeply into ideas about themselves, but most say they never thought they had any of these important internal capacities. However, it has been my experience that as the dialogue deepens, they quickly express deep thinking and feeling about what it means to be spiritual.

As part of a New England Network for Child, Youth, and Family Services survey (Wilson, 2004), I was asked to interview a focus group of young people from seventeen to twenty-three years old in a southern New England mill town who were struggling to live independently, along with other so-called high-risk youth around New England, on the subject of spirituality. They initially scoffed at the idea of spirituality. When we set the context for our hour-and-a-half together as a way to think about the various human dimensions and to talk specifically about spirituality, they became more engaged in dialogue. Open questions about life, death, meaning, and purpose stimulated lively discussion.

The group created its own language around general capacities and on spirituality itself, articulating, for example, how a deceased parent continued to be a guiding force or how a grandmother who went to church all the time had told one burly boy about what she and God see as important things to know in life. Most could find something in their life that they could connect directly or indirectly to this notion of spirit in themselves, or they listened to others with curiosity. Many concluded that it was important to believe in something; while others blurted out that they believed only in themselves because they could not trust anyone else. Their voices reflected increased hope as the dialogue grew louder with belief statements and arguments.

SO HOW IS THIS HELPFUL?

How do we bring this holistic perspective alive within the professions of counseling and education? First, take a moment to consider or even to draw a picture of your whole self. How aware are you of your five dimensions right now (see figure 6.1)? Ask yourself what is profound to you as you look at yourself. Do you feel you are nourishing and balancing your whole self? How do you nourish or support the capacities of those around you?

Now, recall your own adolescence, and write how these dimensions existed for you then. How might having understood yourself in this more holistic way have helped you then?

Thinking self (mind)

Feeling self (heart)

Material self (body/stuff)

Spiritual **self** (nonmaterial)

Social self (family/friends/community)

Perkins 2003

Figure 6.1. Five Dimensions of Self

IMPLICATIONS FOR YOUTH

When we take the time to do the work of self-discovery, we are better able to look at the young people sitting around our dinner table or classroom as holistic beings—full of untapped potential waiting for an opportunity to meet their whole self. We begin to treat them as people on the journey to becoming whole rather than seeing them first as kids with behaviors that are just self-centered, or worse, labeling them as brats. We can help them create opportunities to see, name, and take some responsibility for developing their thinking, feeling, community, material, and spiritual selves in a healthy way.

The spiritual dimension brings us particular challenges with youth. Quite frankly, it brings particular challenges for adults, as well. What will move one person toward his or her spiritual center may be uniquely different from what might move another. The language one uses as an adult may not open a dialogue with youths.

WHAT CAN WE DO?

I have used a variety of practices to help young individuals reach a place within themselves that invites deeper dialogue. Of course, the depth varies by character and age, but when given the opportunity, they go there—into honest self-exploration. A sixteen-year-old girl, at a short workshop called "Discovering Your Spiritual Self" (Perkins, 1997), wrote that her understanding of spirituality is "life and your conscience which is the doorway to God and to your soul and you can find it in anything you see beauty in; love, music, colors, friends, God, thoughts, people, woods, feelings, yourself."

Starting with key educational principles (Vella, 2002) of respect, relevance, and usefulness, we set the stage for asking a sequence of opening questions that deepen the thoughts and feelings associated with a sense of spiritual or deep exploration. Beginning the conversation by quieting the mind through some form of relaxation is very useful. I generally use quieting music and take a few deep breaths.

I often start by naming the five capacities we all have as human beings, asking participants to hold the assumption that we all have these dimensions of the self. From there, we have a context in which to explore the spiritual dimension further. To begin the dialogue, I pose a few provocative questions such as: What happens after you die? What is your calling? Who do you think you really are in this world? Who teaches you how to be in this world? Why care about others? More questions begin to emerge from the group, and the dialogue expands. This is not a time for judging responses, but more for asking additional questions to engage the group more fully in reflection and dialogue about how and why they think or feel a certain way about this inner dimension.

SPIRITUAL MEANING FOR YOUTH

Adolescence is an important time of transition from childhood into adulthood. It is clearly a time of change and new discovery. It is full of predictable cognitive, emotional, physical, social, and even spiritual changes. It is one's first opportunity to use all that has been learned, both tacitly and explicitly, up to this point in life. Adolescents are truly seeking the dynamic balance between what they feel and how they act. If it takes twenty-one repetitions of, say, a precise golf swing in order to master it, will it similarly take many attempts at repeating the desired behaviors, thoughts, and feelings we seek as whole beings?

It is remarkable that adolescents do as well as they do, given the limited support and guidance that our society offers them. Simply being open and willing to listen to a young person wondering about his or her life, reflecting on emotions, thoughts, material needs, community, and the spirituality of adolescence, or recalling one's own adolescent journey helps to strengthen the inner life. This vulnerable and bold path of adolescence is why youths need to deliberately include the spiritual as part of their life experience. They need insightful, experienced, and careful guidance based on the idiosyncratic nature of each individual and what they are uniquely ready for in their exploration.

The adolescent journey can be frustrating and even dangerous. We as parents, educators, and counselors can help adolescents find strength through their internal selves. We must personally feel and know *our own* spiritual selves in order to be in a position to provide support and guidance to adolescents. Be with youths in a safe and honest way so their own spirit or inner life can become a road map for their essential journey. Being in honest communication with caring adults, heart to heart, soul to soul, is a profound and important moment for youths.

My childhood expectation of "never working on Sunday" inspired questions in me. It began my curiosity about what is important beyond the everyday humdrum. I was intrigued by aspects of religion and the questions they raised in me. Others' thoughts and questions about their own growth inspired me to seek new adventures, and the adventures helped to transform many questions into new ideas and meaning for my life. From farming the soil to cultivating my whole self, I had help from others, mostly adults, but most importantly, I reached into my well of inner resources, defined by me as God, love, rightness, honesty, risk, and truth. Imagine what this wondering might mean to other youthful sojourners.

REFERENCES

Bensen, P. L. (1997). *All kids are our kids.* San Francisco: Jossey-Bass.

Goleman, D. (1995). *Emotional intelligence: Why it can matter more than IQ.* New York: Bantam Books.

Hendersen, N. (2007). *Resiliency in action.* Ojai, CA: Resiliency in Action.

James, W. (1952). *The principles of psychology.* Chicago: William Brenton, Encyclopedia Britannica. (Original work published 1890).

Jung, C. (1933) *Modern man in search of a soul.* New York: Harcourt, Brace and World.

Perkins, P. (1991). Human development assessment. (Doctoral disseration). Fielding Institute, Santa Barbara, CA.

———. (1997). *Adolescence: Ah, what a wild time!* (rev. version). Self-published, Calais, VT.

———. (2003). *Five dimensions of the self* (rev. version). Self-published, Calais, VT.

Perkins, P., & Pransky, J. (Eds.). (1994). *Spirituality of Prevention Conference: Participant thoughts and inspirations.* Cabot, VT: Prevention Unlimited.

Pransky, J. (1998). *Modello: A story of hope for the inner city and beyond.* Cabot, VT: NorthEast Health Realization Institute.

Vella, J. (2002). *Learning to listen, learning to teach: The power of dialogue in educating adults.* San Francisco: Jossey-Bass.

Wilson, M. (2004). *A part of you so deep.* Burlington, VT: New England Network for Child, Youth, and Family Services.

II

PRACTICE

7

✛

Deepening Presence
and Interconnection
in the Classroom

Jacqueline Kaufman

They looked expectantly at me or chatted softly, pointing to different books in the neat stack of course texts in front of them. Their notebooks were open, pens held ready to start writing. They were alert, even eager to begin. This was the first January afternoon of my course, "Inner Practices: Deepening Presence and Interconnection in Your Classroom."

"You may limit the class to eight students," I had been told by the director of graduate programs at Vermont's Saint Michael's College. That seemed like a good idea—until I heard from a colleague in an email: "Jackie, did you know that when you told [one student] that your course was closed, she started to cry?"

I reopened enrollment. How could I close the course at eight, or ten, or even sixteen students? I know from direct experience that teachers can learn more about relationships, compassion, and listening through gentle, kind, nonjudgmental inner inquiry than from any amount of in-service hours spent with consultants whose flow charts and PowerPoints guarantee improvement in faculty relationships, school climate, and test scores.

So there, on this darkening January afternoon in 2008, sat seventeen teachers from the Tech Center and the high school where I work, and three additional teachers from other local schools. Each chose from among the wide variety of courses available to educators every semester to be here with me.

I already knew that my description of this course had articulated aspects of their teaching practices that they wanted to explore more deeply. I had written:

> The inner life of the one who teaches is an essential area of inquiry for those in the teaching profession. In order to offer authentic presence and caring to students, the teacher must first offer that to herself. This class engages students in an exploration of personal inner practices that bring a greater awareness of our inner lives and contributes to a pedagogy based on caring and compassion.

This setting, with these students, was an entire world away from my usual teaching practice. For the past fourteen years, I had been a teacher in alternative learning programs across two Vermont counties in four different high schools. What these programs have in common is that they are the last stop for students most at risk of dropping out, most likely to already be patrons of the juvenile justice system, and most able to frustrate the best-intentioned teacher or administrator in the traditional high school setting.

"Alternative ed" is the catch phrase in public education for the programs to which these children are referred for their education. There are currently more than a hundred such programs statewide that take the hardest kids, often with the most difficult lives, and get them "out of the building." By high school, these students have been labeled as problems for a long time, and they certainly know how to embody that description.

Vermont-based holistic educator and publisher Ron Miller (1997) offers this succinct observation of alternative education programs:

> Their main purpose is to make school palatable enough to keep dissatisfied students in the system, not to address the fundamental problems that cause such alienation in the first place. They draw trouble makers and vandals out of the regular school so that the business of education can efficiently continue. (p. 193)

I have grown weary of the extremely demanding alternative setting. Heartbreak and loss usually outweigh accomplishment at year's end. A 50 percent dropout rate is the norm. There is a high percentage of drug use. Parents are stressed, often out of work or on disability, not fond of school, and angry at teachers, and they have lost control of their children. I find myself in the role of counselor and social worker more often than English teacher.

Each year, the students who come to me are younger and more troubled. When I began, I taught seventeen- and eighteen-year-old boys.

Now the population consists mostly of freshman and sophomores and is largely made up of female students. This changing population confirms my belief that something is very wrong with a high school's ability to care, connect, and educate when fourteen-year-olds are sent to an off-campus site within the first few weeks of being in high school. It is one of the reasons I very much wanted to teach teachers. I could positively affect a foundation of caring and compassion for many more students by working directly with their teachers. The other reason is much more personal.

It was many years after I began teaching that my personal journey to find the sacred in myself intersected with my teaching practice. The twists and turns of my own life, and the long shadows of loss and grief, came my way and changed me. Seeking to understand so much pain, I turned, as many do, to a spiritual path. That turn opened me to become more caring, compassionate, and accepting of myself—work that is never complete. And this naturally led to my becoming a quieter, kinder, and more effective teacher.

My path took me to Naropa University's master's program in contemplative education in Boulder, Colorado. This Buddhist-inspired course of studies made me the focus of my work. In a deeply personal, experiential, and intentional manner, I learned how my emotions, associations, and memories are with me in the classroom all of the time. I learned how certain inner practices open me to notice so much more about how I feel and how I tend to react and thus give me the option of choosing to respond from a place of unconditional patience, kindness, and, always, compassion.

Compassion for self and others is the basis for all the practices I learned and embraced. Teaching in a public high school alternative program is a great vehicle for practicing compassion. My students tell me they appreciate that I am calm and do not get angry at them. They come to me when they need someone to listen to them without an agenda, without a rush to judgment about whether they are right or wrong. "You always listen, you always ask good questions or say back to me what you've heard, and then you always give me advice that shows me you love and understand me," one student wrote to me.

Recognizing a growing fatigue in my high school job, I sought, at fifty years old, regeneration rather than the stagnation that psychologist Erik Erikson describes as the final crisis of adult life (see the description of Erikson's stages at http://edtech2.boisestate.edu/vanwagnerk/edtech573/ps07.htm). I wanted to teach teachers what I know about how to go into themselves, their fears, their long-held beliefs, and their neuroses, as well as strengths, with friendliness, kindness, and caring. And I wanted to teach them about bringing what they find first into my graduate course classroom and then into their own classrooms and offices.

Standing in front of that first class that didn't need reminders to settle down or extra time to find a notebook or remember what class they were supposed to be in was new and refreshing. And now it was time for me to begin offering all I know to these twenty expectant, polite, and organized teachers.

I lifted the light wooden ringer of my "singing bowl." This is a brass bowl I bought for myself after graduating from Naropa. In that rigorous program, we had begun and ended every day during the summer intensive with an hour of sitting meditation. The bowl is rung in different patterns to inform those in the hall that meditation is beginning, or that it is time to stand for walking meditation, or that meditation will cease while a teacher gives a talk. I learned to love the ritual of ringing the bowl and the sounds that announced a time to pause, to be silent, to bring awareness to my breath, thoughts, and feelings, and to do nothing.

After my Naropa graduation, I began to use my singing bowl in my own classroom to simply mark the end of the transition between classes and take a small but significant break from the swirl and speed of the school day. I brought the bowl with me this first night of graduate class to do the same—to create some space between the teachers' working day and their transition to being students for the next few hours.

I struck the gleaming bowl three times. When the final pleasant tones dissolved into the room, there was a comfortable silence. I asked my students to push back from their tables, to literally create space between themselves and the work in front of them. I guided them in their first meditation, encouraging a gentle focus on the breath, a soft watchfulness on the nature of the thoughts that run, one after another, like hundreds of fireflies on a warm July night. For ten minutes, my encouragement was to be gentle, to notice, to let go, to come back to the breath, to release tension in the body.

At the close of this modest meditation, they came back to me. Their faces were softer, their body language more relaxed. It was time for me to speak, to offer them the concept of inner practices that would be the foundation of this course.

In that first class, I encouraged those twenty teachers—all of them so prepared to discuss the readings and share their first journal writings—to consider taking time for themselves, ten minutes a day. Anyone who knows teachers, or is a teacher, will recognize that this is a very radical idea, especially when you consider that most teachers are also spouses and parents and are involved in extracurricular activities with students. What I told them was this: "When I speak of inner practices, I mean anything that you do for yourself that brings you peace, joy, quiet delight, strength, courage, or connection. An inner practice can be singing with Aretha or Aerosmith on your commute to school or lighting a candle for ten precious minutes of prayer or meditation before bed or before the morning teakettle sings. Drawing, poetry, making soup with fresh and well-chosen ingredients, sharing silence with the one you love for one hour on a Saturday—all these can be inner practices. My inner practices include solo snowshoeing in the woods and hills around my house, listening to the wind and the trees and the sound of my neighbor raven's wings as he flies above me. What do you do for yourself that connects you with self and spirit? What did you used to do that you just don't feel you have time for anymore?"

The Vietnamese teacher Thich Nhat Hanh (2006) tells us, "Caring for your self, re-establishing peace in yourself, is the basic condition for helping someone else" (p. 47). I explained to the class: "As teachers who give and give to others throughout our days, doesn't that teaching make sense? How can you genuinely care for others, genuinely give to others, if you do not offer that to your own self? That is the encouragement to begin experimenting with inner practices. Ten minutes a day. You deserve ten minutes of your time. You are certainly worthy."

We moved on to the assigned reading from books by Natalie Goldberg, Parker Palmer, Dr. Naomi Remen, and Prof. Mary Rose O'Reilley. I introduced, for the first time that evening, a series of instructions for engaging in conversation that is gentle, slower, and certainly contemplative. *Webster's* defines *contemplative* as "marked by consideration with continued attention." For me, consideration was the key word. I wanted our conversation to be spacious. I wanted everyone to allow more space to truly hear what was being said and to notice the felt response in one's own body. As Palmer wrote in the introduction to O'Reilley's *Radical Presence Teaching as Contemplative Practice* (1998, x): "Don't speak unless you can improve upon the silence."

I asked those who usually speak first to notice that habitual response and wait. I asked those who rarely offer their thoughts and ideas to take the leap, or to pull their journal closer and write what they were feeling and thinking. I asked for some precious seconds of silence after each person spoke to allow for a small settling. I encouraged asking a question about what someone just said instead of offering an opinion or personal continuation of the current thought. I was, through the practice of contemplative conversation developed by Prof. Richard Brown at Naropa University, introducing my new students to the power and possibility of compassion.

I certainly had their attention as I said: "To stay with that impatience or irritation or uncertainty or judgment and getting the knack of relaxing, not rushing to try to change things or fix things or criticize is key to 'slowing down enough to notice what we tend to say and do. The more we witness our emotional chain reactions and understand how they work, the easier it is to refrain' [quoting Pema Chödrön (2000, p. 10)] from jumping in and doing what we have always done in the past. This is the beginning of clarity, of being awake and open to ourselves. And if you are not awake and open to yourself, how can you offer that to others?"

As our first class continued, some students who often speak first spoke first. Others changed their bodies' positions in their blue plastic chairs to those of listener: they leaned back, cocked their heads to one side, the hand holding the pen or pencil resting alongside the open notebook page. I noticed that others pulled their journals toward them to take note in the moment on an idea, an emotion, a judgment to reflect on later. What I felt in that first class was a willingness to engage with the work that was as appealing and refreshing as the hot green tea and homemade oatmeal cookies I had set out earlier on a table at the rear. We were coming together in a new way in just under two hours.

Oh, there was skepticism at that table! And there was the fear and insecurity and attraction and aversion that all human beings feel and think in any given moment. More important to me, we were beginning to pay attention to how we felt in our bodies and thought in our minds, and just beginning to notice our habitual responses to both. We were preparing the ground to grow into a caring, compassionate, and contemplative community.

On an inspiration, I ended that first class in a way that became our closing ritual. I handed the singing bowl to one class member, who had been consistently fearless in the yoga class we shared. I asked her to speak her intention for that ten-minute inner practice she would do over the next seven days.

She smiled and took the bowl. She gazed into its golden center. "I will take ten minutes at school to be less hectic." She tentatively struck the bowl. Everyone sat with quiet respect. The bowl went to the person to her right. "I am going to read for pleasure," this one promised. Around the bowl went. "I am going to try understanding if I am happy." "I am going to practice yoga." "I am going to spend time outside by myself." "I am going to get back to meditating."

Occasionally someone fumbled with the striker or whether to hold the bowl in one hand or put it on the table. Others hit the inside of the rim instead of the roundness of the bowl. Their shoulders hunched, they laughed at themselves and either quickly gave the bowl to the next person or asked the group, "How do I do this?" Once answered by others, those teachers made the bowl sing again. "I am going to feed the birds and watch them." "I am going to use my chimes of compassion." "I am going to spend time with my horse every day." "I am going to reflect on what I am grateful for in my life." "I am going to write just for myself." "I am going to dance like a crazy woman." "I am going to read to my daughter and plan my garden."

Finally, the bowl came back to me. I allowed the words to settle inside the bowl and in each of us. I realized that the teachers in this room had lost something precious somewhere through their years of negotiating the pressures, expectations, and speed of the school year: they had lost the ability to be still, to give to themselves, to recognize the importance of taking a very small part of their time just for themselves to do as they please. If they could stay with their newly spoken intention to do that, I believed they would find long-missed parts of themselves. I rang my bowl three times and as the tones faded into the evening, I thanked everyone for a wonderful first class.

The next day I began to receive emails from my colleague students. Here are two excerpts:

> I think I am going to really benefit from taking the time to look at myself and the way I teach. I've used the breathing twice during class and I could not believe how much it helped to calm myself and give the students space to answer, get back on task, connect to the material.

> I knew right away that it [this class] was going to address some of the things that I desperately need to look at. Horses smell good in winter sun.

"How did you ever get twenty more different teachers in that class?" a guidance counselor asked me one day a few weeks into the course. The range of men and women included a rural middle school teacher, high school tech teachers, guidance counselors, and a secondary school teacher of the year. I didn't do anything but offer a different, deeper, and more personal conversation that resonated for twenty different reasons.

In class, I asked my students to close their eyes and eat unknown foods I placed in their hands, and then to draw what they tasted—not the thing itself or its name. In another class, I brought in long banners of black cotton and asked them to draw circles on it with colored chalk and then—without thinking, but feeling it in their hearts—to write in the center of their circle the one word that described what was most alive in the center of their classrooms. *Integrity, community, caring, respect, belonging, discovery,* and *knowledge* were some of the words that entered those circles.

I consistently carried on the ritual of setting out hot tea and fresh cookies before their arrival. I began each class with a brief relaxation meditation or stretching period. Before discussion of the readings, I reminded everyone of the guidelines for contemplative conversation that created the space to truly hear and notice one's physical and intellectual response before reacting. And we always closed with each student speaking a question, a resonance, an observation, or a fear over the singing bowl and then striking it so the tone carried their words throughout all of us. The changes I began to see and read about were small, simple, and yet profound.

There was a gentling of our space as we collectively recognized the community being created on Tuesday afternoons. "The masks are beginning to come off," read one email I received. There was space to think, to be heard, or just to breathe. There were more questions asked of those who spoke to pull out deeper insights.

I noticed a diminishing tendency to bring conversations around to anecdotes and war stories from their classrooms. My students were more willing to allow for pauses before responding, a sign of deeper listening. They became more courageous about sharing writings from their course papers and even personal journal entries about their heightened awareness of being present in their lives and their classrooms. They spoke about the difficulties and rewards of working with inner practices at home and at school to become more available, more present in the moment with themselves and their students. My students were finding out for themselves the benefits of "going in and in and turn[ing] away from nothing" (Faulds, 1997, p. 6) This course was working on a very deep and personal level because that is where the students chose to go.

For me, there were some awakenings in the difference between teaching recalcitrant teens and motivated teachers. The teachers all wanted As and made their cases for better grades—something I had never encountered. In my first outing as professor, this made me go back to my course requirements and carefully compare their work with what I expected. There were the standard expectations around meeting deadlines, coming to class, writing papers in APA style. More important were the guidelines around contemplative conversation and the traits that I referred to in midsemester written evaluations of each student, including detailed examples of my expectations for generosity, discipline, patience, and kindness. I thought the percentages allotted to aspects of the syllabus would serve as guidelines for grades. The persistence from some students in deviating from the guidelines has prompted me to create a very clear and lengthy course rubric that I can now simply refer them to when they question their grades.

Some students came to the realization on their own that there really is no difference between what we are inside and how we present outside. Others needed more guidance and direction to recognize that reality. I intend to spend more time on that aspect of the course. I look forward to creating exercises and assignments that bring students' inner work more explicitly into their daily work.

My students seemed genuinely happy to see each other and me each week. Their joy in their inner practices and the increasing confidence in developing a more complete presence in their work with students grew along with their proficiency in using the singing bowl. Listen to their words, written in their response papers:

> For the last several years I have been focused on curriculum and instruction. Through my inner practices, I began to realize that what I was teaching was

the curriculum and not the students. This needed to change. . . . Now I ask how I can help them and try not to insert my agenda into their time with me. My tone has lightened and softened and I talk slower. I talk less. Because of this, I am able to change the way I listen to my students. I also pay attention to how they are speaking to me. As I focus on the "self that teaches" I realize how uptight I've been. I have noticed that being more relaxed does not mean getting less done. I still get everything accomplished but I am enjoying life more. We are all smiling more.

So often I have gotten caught up in the whirlwind, forgetting to be present, letting the confusion rule my day. I had forgotten to be present with myself or I just didn't know how. I find myself now with a natural calmness that has taken me by surprise and sometimes I cannot give it a name.

My inner practices can give me the strength, clarity, courage and flexibility to pursue my difficult [work] with integrity and real presence to the dilemma at hand. In order to be really present I need to keep an open heart and mind about the outcome. As Kessler so aptly reminds us, "Our heart can become blocked also when we are attached to a particular plan, technique or approach in the classroom. If we can keep our hearts open, we see the unique needs of our students and discover an entirely different way to reach our larger goals. This capacity to care deeply about our students and our mission, without being attached to a specific, 'known' outcome on a given day, is crucial to the art of being fully present" [quoting from Rachael Kessler, "The Teaching Presence," at http://passageworks.org/wp-content/uploads/file/UnpublishedTeach-ing Presence.pdf].

Developing an inner practice reminds me that we all need to work on these things everyday. It makes me stop and think, challenge my assumptions and give myself permission to take the time to be present. When I can do this, it gives me time and space to slow the world down a bit. . . . I can become present, pull myself into integration and then take appropriate action. I can tell when this is purposeful and thoughtful. It is accepted and appreciated. As Boorstein writes, "given enough space, support and encouragement, the heart calms down—and wakes up—all by itself."

As the semester lengthened, so did the amount of light in the early spring sky. I walked into sunshine even after I completed my personal end-of-class rituals. I washed all the teacups. I offered any leftover cookies to the woman on the cleaning crew who each week patiently waited for me to leave so she could get on with her night's work. I hauled all the class materials to my car and often sat for a few moments to record my own experience of the class, such as this observation:

For me, this class had become a refuge and a wonder. What they write is so beautiful. They listen and open and follow me, just another flawed human being. They move me so with their inspiration and courage. All I had to do was offer this conversation, these wise readings and they fly. They soar. I look up from the ground where I stand and watch them with such awe.

REFERENCES

Chödrön, P. (2001). *The places that scare you: A guide to fearlessness in difficult times.* Boston: Shambhala Classics.

Faulds, D. (1997). *Go in and in: More poems from the heart of yoga.* Kearney, NE: Morris.

Hanh, Thich Nhat. (2006). *True love: A practic for awakening the heart.* Boston: Shambhala Books.

Miller, R. (1997). *What are schools for? Holistic education in American culture.* Brandon, VT: Holistic Education Press.

O'Reilley, M. R. (1998). *Radical presence teaching as contemplative practice.* Portsmouth, NH: Boynton Cook.

8

The Yogi in the Classroom

Donald Tinney

W hen I was a boy learning to play hockey at the Bobby Orr–Mike Walton Sports Camp in Orillia, Ontario, I chose the position of defenseman, which meant that I spent much of my time skating backward, trying to stop opponents from getting a clear shot at the goal. Most young defensemen make the mistake of reaching for the puck on the opponent's stick, so a common expression shouted in any rink is "Play the man!" If the defender stops the *player*, another teammate can take care of the puck.

The best coaching advice about this strategy I received came from a college player who was running me through some drills. "Just keep watching my chest; that will tell you where I'm going," he said, crossing the blue line on his way to take a shot. He explained that a player can make a head fake—pretending to look in one direction, then skating in another— or move his hands in a confusing manner to trick the defender, but it is physically impossible for an athlete to not follow in the same direction as his chest, the home of the heart.

I learned that lesson nearly forty years ago and only recently realized that it is also a valuable lesson for teaching. I can give my students a head fake, the intellectual equivalent of the bob-and-weave, but the direction of my chest—my heart—determines the direction of my pedagogy. My heart determines the quality of the teaching and learning in my classroom.

While my hockey career was a brief one, I went on to participate in other sporting activities—football, tennis, running, kayaking—and as I entered my thirties, began strength training in an attempt to keep in shape and stave off the effects of aging. Ten years ago, one of my gym buddies convinced me to skip weightlifting one evening to try a yoga class held in the aerobics room. I have practiced yoga ever since.

Before I tried that one class, I held the typical American male point of view on yoga, which was based on complete ignorance of the practice. While I cannot imagine my life without yoga now, I doubt if I would have tried a single class if my friend hadn't talked me into giving it a shot. Rodney Yee (2002), one of America's most popular yoga teachers, explains that my attitude and early yoga experiences were fairly typical.

> Why do you think there are not very many men in yoga class? Because of one big factor, and that is that they think that yoga class is about flexibility, and most men have the image of themselves that they're really quite stiff. But really where they're stiff is in their head. . . .
>
> I would say that's the number one reason why most men haven't been in yoga class—because they think that they won't be very competent at it. . . .
>
> Men are actually very strongly into body image, even though in some ways their body image comes from the capability of doing a sport rather than from the shape of their body. So that's where yoga intimidates them because, in some sense, their body actually doesn't function very well. (pp. 19–20)

The ego-threatening, physical awkwardness of my first few yoga classes almost made me quit the practice for good, but I stayed with it and received important lessons about growing comfortable in my own body and about being a humble man. American boys are raised to be competitive, to be the winner, the biggest, and the best, but there is nothing to win in yoga class, so competition does not exist there. In addition to that general reality, I practice at a yoga studio in a college town, so during any given class I could be surrounded by coeds young enough to be my daughters and flexible enough to be accomplished gymnasts, so comparing myself to them—let alone competing with them—would not only be counterproductive, it would be demoralizing and depressing.

Americans are obsessed with competition. Boys of my generation were encouraged to participate in competitive athletics because it would prepare us for the dog-eat-dog business world. Today, I see the value of competitive athletics in the opportunities to be a member of a team, to find a mentor in a coach, and to learn how to cooperate with others in working toward a common goal. But beating the opponent is one of the least significant parts of the entire experience.

This same competitive attitude infuses our classrooms, as well. Any teacher who passes back tests and papers during class has heard the echoes of "What did you get?" I believe it is my responsibility to create a classroom environment which is noncompetitive; competition constantly leads to comparison between—and judgments of—students, which is counterproductive to learning. In many ways, I attempt to create a classroom environment that is similar to one of my yoga classes.

I have been blessed with a number of gifted yoga teachers who have taught me as much about the art of teaching and the art of living as I have ever learned in a college classroom. These compassionate, committed, and gentle teachers have been role models for me, despite the fact that I am older than all of them. A quality they all share is that they are calm and quiet people, reminding me that teachers need not be loud and boisterous. I know that I talk too much in the classroom and take little comfort in knowing that most other teachers talk too much, as well. Teachers are challenged to manage their students' learning activities without dominating the classroom and the conversation.

Every yoga teacher I have had experience with has reminded every class that our practice is our *own* practice, personalized and individualized by us alone. They offer suggestions and provide demonstrations for various asana postures, but the position in which we put our bodies is ultimately our own decision. My yoga teachers do not exercise any authority over us as students. Donna Farhi (2003) explains the importance of this approach:

> However helpful any teacher has been, it is crucial that we not insert an outside authority within ourselves. When we do so, we tend to strive to have the experience we think we should have, and thus there is nothing we have discovered ourselves—nothing original or authentic. As Krishnamurti puts it, we become "secondhand people," having secondhand experiences. (p. 114)

As a teacher, I want my authority to live in my compassion and my clarity, not in my position. As a teacher of writing, I know that students are stifled when they attempt to write for the authority figures of teachers or professors. Their writing, as Farhi points out, becomes far less authentic as they write the teacher's essay, not their own.

To avoid imposing or inserting authority in the classroom, I rely on my yoga practice, as well as on life experiences that some might call a spiritual journey, to remind myself that I am a compassionate, caring, powerful, and loving man. Teachers who do not accept their own goodness and their own magnificence rely on their institutional authority—grade books, assignments, penalties, threats of calling parents, test scores—to control their students.

If I were an English teacher who loves power and control more than I love my students, then I would expect my students to accept and understand *my* interpretation and analysis of a piece of literature rather than expecting them to generate *their own* analysis and interpretation. However, while the process might take longer and appear less efficient, I want my students to ask their own questions, not just attempt to answer mine. Krishnamurti (1996) explores the importance of learning being based on the students' questions:

> To experience what is solitude and what is meditation, one must be in a state of inquiry; only a mind that is in a state of inquiry is capable of learning. But when inquiry is suppressed by previous knowledge, or by the authority and experience of another, then learning becomes mere imitation, and imitation causes a human being to repeat what is learned without experiencing it.
>
> Teaching is not the mere imparting of information but the cultivation of an inquiring mind. (p. 99)

During the early stages of my yoga practice, I was somewhat confused by one of the remarks my teachers would regularly make at the start of each class: "Bring to mind an intention for your practice." I confused *intention* with an objective I might have for one of my classes—something to be accomplished, a standard to be met. The intention of a yoga practice is not about accomplishment, though; it is about the union of mind, body, and spirit, as writer and yoga teacher Jeff Davis (2004) explains:

> Before practicing yoga, I set an intention. An intention is a conscious gesture to align your mind, heart, imagination, and body with whatever act you're about to begin—whether it's a series of physical poses, breathing awareness, a day of karma yoga and good acts, or a writing session. (p. 4)

My classes always go more smoothly when I take the time for the inner practice of setting an intention for each session. These meditations last only a few seconds, but they can shift my experience: I will be at peace. I will listen. This is a calm place. I will see everyone here. We will laugh today.

To have students practice setting their own intentions, I ask them to write in their journals in response to a simple question, "What will you create today?" Students need to know that they create their own experience in the classroom and create their own value for that experience.

I emphasize the fact that setting an intention takes only seconds, for I know that most teachers will argue that they don't have time to engage in one more activity. We teachers tend to have an unhealthy relationship with time and always seem to be rushing through assignments and units to meet various institutional demands. A healthy inner practice demands that we slow down the hectic pace found in most schools. One way to accomplish this is to engage in breath awareness exercises, called *pranayama* in yoga. Simply paying attention to one's breath will lead to a slower pace, a human pace. "Slowing down is the precursor to yoga practice because this simple act allows us to consider our thoughts, feelings, and actions more carefully in the light of our desire to live peacefully," writes Farhi (2003, p. 53).

In my English classes, I find that silent reading and journal writing are two exercises that effectively slow the pace for students; both activities bring calm and peace to the classroom. When surveyed, my students consistently say that the independent reading time is one of their favorite activities of the course. They appreciate having the time to be quiet during their busy days and to read a book of their own choosing. We rarely offer our students or ourselves periods of extended silence. I believe that schools are too noisy—a problem exacerbated by the addition of iPods and cell phones.

Psychotherapist and yoga teacher Stephen Cope believes that a practice of silence is the only way to get underneath untruth, as explained by Swami Kripalu: "Silence is the first step toward obtaining truth since it helps us to curb untruth, which we generally express by talking excessively all day. This incessant flood of speech makes us prone to the bad habit of speaking untruth" (quoted in Cope, 2006, p. 160). Cope points out that yogis are not the only ones who have discovered the value of silence:

> In the Native American tradition, when a young man set out to find the vision that would direct and give meaning to his life, he would leave his people to fast in solitude and silence. In silence the Spirit would come and speak to him. He would return home full of the Spirit—quieter on the outside, more full of life on the inside. "Guard your tongue in youth," advised the Lakota chief Wabashaw, "and in age you may mature a thought that will be of service to your people." (p. 160)

One result of my practice of silence in the classroom has been that I have become a better listener. If I am not eager to fill the space with the sound of my own voice, I can take the time to listen to my students. They will not speak with ease or eagerness at first, but they want to be heard. Exercising patience and finding comfort with silence has allowed me to pose a question or two and then simply wait for a response from a student who will actually begin the class discussion. If we do not listen to our students, how can we know them? And if we don't know them, how can we support them in their learning? As Krishnamurti (1996) points out, listening is not an easy task.

> There is an art of listening. To be able to really listen, one should abandon or put aside all prejudices, preformulations, and daily activities. When you are

in a receptive state of mind, things can be easily understood; you are listening when your real attention is given to something. But unfortunately most
of us listen through a screen of resistance. We are screened with prejudices,
whether religious or spiritual, psychological, or scientific; or with our daily
worries, desires, and fears. (p. 60)

The harried classroom teacher worried about test scores, state standards, attendance, hall passes, and committee meetings will be challenged to practice the important art of listening. I find it necessary to engage in some sort of quieting or grounding practice (setting an intention)
early in the class to clear my own mind and spirit enough to allow me to
be an effective listener. If I do not listen to my students, I cannot inspire
my students.

While listening, I need to remind myself that I am not listening to
find mistakes and errors. I am not there to pass judgment; I am there to
be a sounding board and to support students in developing their ideas.
One of the most appealing aspects of yoga class for me is the absence of
judgment. Being present in the moment does not allow for judgment,
since one is focused on one's breath and experience of one's own body,
not comparing oneself to other yogis or to some unattainable standard. I
strive for a similar presence in the classroom, focusing on the ideas students are expressing and highlighting the strengths of their arguments.

Many teachers, particularly content-driven high school teachers, scoff
at pedagogy that embraces the spiritual dimension of education or the
language of the heart, writing it off as being touchy-feely, undisciplined,
and based on emotions. My practice of yoga has led me to see this approach as anything but that, as Farhi (2003) points out: "Unlike Western
models of psychology and therapy, yoga does not place great stakes in
feelings. Because of their transitory nature, neither positive nor negative
feelings can be an accurate representation of the wisdom mind" (p. 212).
Too often we give our students permission to let their emotions run, and
sometimes ruin, their lives. When we teach from our hearts, we don't allow this to happen. When students complain to me that they don't like
a book I've assigned, my response is simple: The book doesn't care. The
study of literature, like Farhi's practice of yoga, is not about a student's
feelings; it is about a student's ability to construct meaning through interpretation and analysis.

As do yoga teachers, we have a responsibility to support our students
as they learn that they are the masters of their emotions, as Cope (2003)
explains:

Where there is greed, we can systematically train the heart toward generosity. Where there is anger, we can train the heart toward loving kindness.
Where there is jealousy and envy, we can train the heart toward sympathetic

joy. Where there is hatred, train toward compassion—and so forth. In the yoga tradition, each afflictive emotion has its own "opposite" or "antidote" which can be intentionally cultivated. (p. 177)

I enjoyed my involvement with Jacqueline Kaufman's graduate course and found my colleagues to be a supportive group on a professional and personal level. Without it ever being articulated, I think our class developed four attitudes about social relationships, as explained by Farhi (2003):

These qualities of the heart are conducive to peace of mind and thus can enable us to overcome the distractions that already exist in the mind and to prevent the production of more psychological distress. They are:

1. Friendliness toward the joyful
2. Compassion for those who are suffering
3. Celebrating the good in others
4. Remaining impartial to the faults and imperfections of others (p. 99)

I am grateful for my practice of yoga and for the opportunity to work and study with my colleagues, which has allowed me to articulate the connections I have drawn between teaching English and practicing yoga. If there is one single inner practice that will lead to success as a teacher, it is the practice of gratitude. If we do not live in a state of gratitude, then we will live in a state of victimization. Being grateful for my students in every class allows me to see them as the magnificent beings they are and allows me to be the teacher I am becoming.

REFERENCES

Cope, S. (2006). *The wisdom of yoga: A seeker's guide to extraordinary living*. New York: Bantam Dell.

Davis, J. (2004). *The journey from the center to the page: Yoga philosophies and practices as muse for authentic writing*. New York: Penguin.

Farhi, D. (2003). *Bringing yoga to life: The everyday practice of enlightened living*. New York: HarperCollins.

Krishnamurti, J. (1996). *Total freedom: The essential Krishnamurti*. New York: Harper-Collins.

Yee, R. (2002). *Yoga: The poetry of the body*. New York: St. Martin's Press.

9

Simple in Means,
Rich in Ends

Sara Caldwell

For years, I had wanted to fall in love with teaching, to find the passion for it and to believe that it truly is the profession for me. I couldn't quite put a finger on what was missing until I took a course called "Inner Practices: Deepening Presence and Interconnection in the Classroom." What drew me to the course were the words *inner*, *presence*, and *connection*. My inner world of feeling and knowing the sacredness in all things did not match my outer world of grade expectations and assessments. I didn't know how to bring this inner life into the classroom, or even that I could or should. I didn't know how to let the sacredness of my students, myself, and the world seep into and out of my teaching.

My presence in the classroom was not truly authentic; I felt that I had to leave the emotional and spiritual parts of myself at the door. I was guarded, stiff, lacking joy, and even a bit sad. I heard, but did not listen with my heart; I talked, but did not speak with compassion; I cared, but was not cared for. And because of all this, my ability to create the space for interconnection was severely diminished. I wasn't able to be a good teacher in the way that I understood good teachers to be, which is to "possess a capacity for connectedness" and to "offer up soul, or self-hood, as the loom on which to weave a fabric of connectedness between themselves, their students, their subjects, and the world" (Palmer, 2001, p. 132). I wanted desperately to be that kind of teacher, but something was getting in the way, and I needed, for my students and me, to find out what that was.

I began to ask myself what was missing. What I discovered was guilt about being a teacher in a public school. The critic within told me that I was contributing to and feeding our cultural paradigm of devaluing and disassociating heart and spirit from mind and body. I felt that I was doing the students an extreme disservice by not focusing equally on them in their entirety, that I was teaching them to be imbalanced by addressing only their mental and physical intelligences. I felt that teaching wasn't good enough, noble enough, or sacred enough to fulfill me in my entirety. Isolated and seemingly alone with my hope that teaching could nourish all parts of me, I put those soul and spirit parts of myself away during the day, only to realize that when I let them out again, they were starving.

I was tired without knowing why and had forgotten the reason I went into teaching in the first place. Increasingly disheartened, both the students and I grew more bored, restless, and rigid, and less spontaneous, curious, and joyful. I imagined this was not only my story but also the story of teachers everywhere.

As Parker Palmer (1998) says, "The health of education depends on our ability to hold sacred and secular together so that they can correct and enrich each other" (p. 111). I had always understood that the role of education was to lead out and bring forth the uniqueness and potential of students, which to me means nurturing the whole child—mind, body, and spirit. In this way, the sacred and the secular are essentially inseparable and cannot be addressed in isolation if true education is to take place. If this was my belief for students, it must also be a belief I hold for myself. Aostre Johnson (1999) asks the essential question:

> How can we as educators help make our students whole if we are not committed to becoming whole ourselves? We have to ask what stands in the way of each of us becoming wholly ourselves. . . . We become more ourselves by letting go, discovering the holy working in and through us as we live with others. It is this willingness to engage deeply and honestly in the process of self-discovery and personal change, in community with others, that is sometimes called spiritual growth. (p. 108)

The first step in my journey toward truly loving to teach was to create space in my life. I had to discover what was standing in my way of being whole. I had to start doing some "soul work."

The process of getting to know my soul again had to include some way of giving attention to the details of my senses and the threads that my emotions follow. I committed to a daily practice of giving myself five to ten minutes each morning to just breathe, to notice my thoughts and sensations, and then to let it all drift away. As I did this over time, I could see the patterns and the threads that make up who I am. Sometimes I found that the child within me needed mothering, and that's why I felt sad. Or the child within just wanted to play, but felt like she couldn't because I had to act "professional." Other times, I found that the rebel in me wanted to break all the rules I've been taught and that I teach, and that's why I felt restless and frustrated. The mother in me felt tired from giving and giving, but rarely truly receiving.

By seeing and honoring these parts of myself, I began to cultivate a strong sense of my own identity, and in the process was coming to deeply know my soul. By sitting in silence, I became open enough to claim the events of my life, all of them—good, bad, and everything in between. "You only need to claim the events of your life to make yourself yours. When you truly possess all you have been and done, you are fierce with reality" (Scott-Maxwell, 1983, p. 42).

I came to have a sense of compassion for myself as my humanness came into view and I finally began to reclaim and "re-member" my mind, body, and soul. A practice that puts us back in touch with our own soul is the foundation necessary for touching the souls of others. Thich Nhat Hanh (2006) reflects this when saying: "Caring for yourself, re-establishing peace in yourself is the basic condition for helping someone else" (p. 47).

After ten weeks of this practice, I wrote this in my journal:

> I feel like I am much more astute at communicating from both heart and mind, instead of just mind; and as a result, there is space within my interactions for compassion to come. I'm not saying it happens every time, but what I notice is that a student will say or do something that is difficult to deal with and instead of reacting, I go into the feeling tone of his or her words and ask several question simultaneously: Is this anger, fear, joy, shame, frustration, need of love, pride, or sadness? Then, if I can name the emotion and where it lives inside of me, I can let it go because I've got that too, and who am I to judge or react with fear, scorn, disdain, frustration, or anger?
>
> For me, compassion comes when I can, in some way, imagine walking in their shoes. The only way that I can know this is to pay attention to the thoughts and feelings that arise from within me, to name them, to validate them, and then let them go. Because of my inner practice, I realize how much I love humanness, my own and my students', and that's what makes it easier to deal with those difficult moments.

As a result of this soul work, very simple in means but rich in ends, I can now learn to care for and nurture all parts of myself and to give that caring to students—but what about teaching the students to do the same? In order for true caring to take place, I wanted to give them the opportunity to learn how to do it for themselves, with the hope that it would eventually allow their vibrant wholeness to come out, therefore returning to my original reason for teaching: to heal our culture's fear of addressing emotional and spiritual intelligence in schools. As Nel Noddings (1992) explains:

> A *caring relation* is, in its most basic form, a connection or encounter between two human beings—a carer and a recipient of care, or cared-for. In order for the relation to be properly called caring, both parties must contribute to it in characteristic ways. A failure on the part of either carer or cared-for blocks completion of caring and, although there may still be a relation—that is, an encounter or connection in which each party feels something toward the other—it is not a *caring* relation. (p. 15)

I wanted my students to contribute to the relationship as fully as they could, bringing love of their own identity and care for all parts of themselves as human beings into the dynamic of the classroom. And, to be honest, I also wanted to allow myself to be cared for by them. This seemed overwhelming, but I started anyway. I decided to share a simple form of my inner practice with the sixth grade. I began by telling them that I had been doing some wonderful work in a class that I was taking that helped me to know myself more deeply and fully than I ever had before. This sparked their interest, I think, because they had thought that all adults know exactly who they are, never changing or growing. I became vulnerable in front of them, and it felt so freeing to share at such a deep level with them.

I showed them how to be silent, to breathe, and to watch their thoughts. I told them that by watching their thoughts, they could see their personalities—their obsessions, fears, hopes, desires, and loves. I told them about some of my thought patterns, the ones that seem to come a thousand times a day, the shallow ones and the deep ones. I taught them the concept of *nonjudgment*, especially of themselves. I told them that what I do is put unwanted thoughts on a leaf and watch it just float down the river, opening myself to a new pattern of thoughts, to creativity. I told them that they create themselves through the thoughts that they have, and that to become aware of these thoughts is the first step toward understanding who they are.

They were eager to try it themselves, so I set aside five minutes each day, right after lunch and recess, for this meditative practice. After about three weeks of doing this together, I had them journal about how it was going. Here are some of their responses:

- "The class isn't meditating like everybody assumes, not sitting crossed legged and saying 'ohm' but actually just sitting at the tables and putting heads down and releasing all thoughts. . . . It might be the rest that everyone gets from the meditation; then again, releasing thoughts means releasing stressful ideas or memories. . . . It is changing the class in a splendid way."

- "It also helps me with my fear of knowing if my work is good or not."
- "The meditation creates a blank, absentness in my mind that I didn't even think was possible. Yet, it helps me get to know myself and what my personality is like. Every wandering thought—worries, fears, joys, anxiety, envy, despair, laughs—each one that I let float away gives me a clue to what I'm like."
- "The meditation seems to help me calm down from recess and be ready to work. Reading class changed from a B+ to an A+."
- "When I meditate all my thoughts and worries disappear. And when I do my work at school, all the answers come to me."
- "It helps me focus on my inner self and gives me an opportunity to let all my feelings and thoughts go. I have noticed that meditation relieves pressure and my schoolwork is a lot better than it usually was. I get a chance to feel soothed and confident!"
- "After our five minute meditation I feel ready for anything that comes my way."
- "Meditation helps me calm down and think things through later on."
- "It is kind of like my mind is a dirty car and then when I go through the meditation it is like a car wash."
- "I'm not into or attached to the learning. . . . This is just time to do nothing."
- "I can think more clearly and make smarter decisions more easily."

Five minutes is not a long time, yet the outcome was tremendous. These students were now much more eager to learn, asking deeper thinking questions, and much more caring toward each other. I am more energetic, spontaneous, and happy in the classroom than I have ever been. Connections are being made all the time now—connections within the mind and, even more powerfully, connections of the heart. I think the students are feeling much more comfortable, much more expressive of themselves, and are learning at a deeper level. The soul has been invited in. Masks and walls that we put up to protect ourselves have dropped away, and I can characterize the presence in the classroom as genuine. In Rachael Kessler's (2001) words:

> When soul enters the classroom, students venture to share the joy and talents they might have feared would provoke jealousy in even their best friends. They dare to risk exposing the pain or shame that might be judged as weakness. Seeing deeply into the perspectives of others, accepting what has felt unworthy in themselves, students discover compassion and begin to learn about forgiveness. Inviting soul into education means giving students the skills to dive down into the deep well that is unique to each individual, and to meet at the underground stream that connects all wells. (p. 111)

In sharing my story, I do not mean to say that my students and I are present and authentic all the time, or that each moment in the classroom is joyful and profound, but instead wanted to show how something as simple as giving ourselves five minutes a day to learn how to go inside and find out what we feel can lead to such a change in our experience. Knowing ourselves intimately, without unkind judgment, and acting with authenticity and compassion helps to feed us. I now understand my work as a public school teacher to be sacred and healing, not only for my students, my community, and myself but also for a system of education that is long overdue for a shift toward wholeness.

REFERENCES

Johnson, A. N. (1999). Teaching as sacrament. In Kincheloe, J. L., Steinberg, S. R., & Villaverde, L. E. (Eds.), *Rethinking intelligence: Confronting psychological assumptions about teaching and learning*. New York: Routledge. 106–1114

Kessler, R. (2001). Soul of students, soul of teachers: Welcoming the inner life to school. In Lantieri, L. (Ed.), *Schools with spirit: Nurturing the inner lives of children and teachers*. Boston: Beacon. 108–113

Nhat Hanh, T. (2006). *True love: A practice for awakening the heart*. Boston: Shambhala.

Noddings, N. (1992). *The challenge to care in schools: An alternative approach to education*. New York: Teacher's College Press.

Palmer, P. J. (1998). *The courage to teach: Exploring the inner landscape of a teacher's life*. San Francisco: Jossey-Bass.

Palmer, P. J., with Jackson, M., Jackson, R., & Sluyter, D. (2001). The courage to teach: A program for teacher renewal. In Lantieri, L. (Ed.), *Schools with spirit: Nurturing the inner lives of children and teachers*. Boston: Beacon. 132–147

Scott-Maxwell, F. (1983). *The measure of my days*. New York: Penguin.

10

The Inner Life of Teaching

Joyce Kemp

With a little trepidation, and more than a bit of excitement, I enrolled in a new course offering called "Inner Practices: Deepening Presence and Interconnection in the Classroom." I knew the person teaching the course and knew it would be challenging—not necessarily from the amount of paperwork involved, but I knew we would be taking a long, hard look at ourselves as people and as educators. Obviously, just from the name of the course, I expected to do some inner work, but I didn't know just how that work would affect my classroom life. I wrote in my journal and first reflection paper that I had "been on an interesting journey for the past several years, concentrating on my inner self—trying to come to a place of peace, where I am kind and compassionate to others and myself. I believe this class was given to me as part of this journey." "Inner Practices" took my hand and guided me through a leg of my journey, and taught me more than I expected it would. That part of the voyage was enlightening, entertaining, and difficult at times. But it helped me grow as both a person and an educator.

The first thing we worked on was presence. We focused on being "in the moment," which allows us to be more available to our students and the subject at hand. As I wrote at the time:

> I realized one day last week that I have really not been present for my
> students; that I'm constantly thinking ahead, often formulating an answer
> while the question is still being asked, or thinking about what's going to
> happen—what am I going to say next, what are we going to do tomorrow or
> next week. . . . No wonder I can't relax into my teaching!

We first simply focused on our breathing for several minutes at a time to create a calmness and relaxation of thought. We continued throughout the first several weeks of class with "intentional breathing," created an inner practice for ourselves (mine was meditation for ten minutes each day—others wrote, played, or simply had a cup of tea early in the morning before others in their household were awake), and then practiced deeply listening to one another. All of these experiences helped me to pay attention to my students and to myself. I am now more present in all matters with all people. "What we say in our encounters is less important than how present we are able to be" (O'Reilley, 1998, p. 31).

I believe that I have become a more compassionate person just by being present. As I put it in my journal:

> What's happening now is that I'm more present than I have ever been in
> the classroom. I certainly still have times when I'm fretting about what to
> say next, what we're going to do next week, or what I'm having for dinner.
> But every once-in-a-while I catch myself feeling like I'm in this fabulous
> place—everything is as it should be, things are flowing, and it feels GOOD!
> I also find that I'm hearing what my students are saying to me (verbally and
> non-verbally) and I actually like them a lot more than I did before! I also
> like myself a whole lot more—as a person and as a teacher. As I'm getting
> to know and accept myself, I'm feeling more connected to my students and
> my teaching.

The experience of presence has allowed me to see my students as whole and complete individuals. Because of this, I have become a more compassionate teacher.

"Compassion emerges from a sense of belonging: the experience that all suffering is like our suffering and all joy is like our joy. When we know ourselves to be connected to all others, acting compassionately is simply the natural thing to do" (Glazer, 1999, p. 34). This connectedness and compassion has helped me begin to find my voice, and to relax into my teaching by creating space for my students as well as myself.

One example of compassion that I have noticed on a grand scale has to do with a former student. It appeared to me that this student felt superior to the others in class, complained about the workload, and was quick to berate others. I didn't really give this student a chance for the first half of the year. I realized I was grading this student's projects more harshly and was not inviting the student into conversation during our work time in class. Deepening my presence in the classroom by two-minute breathing breaks during the day, I started looking at all students in a different way. When I took off the dark glasses of my own "unexamined shadows" (Palmer, 1998, p. 2), I began to see that this student was human, too—that much of the tough outer shell was a cover for insecurities. I see now that I was not teaching, not giving students what they needed, by not feeling connected. Showing compassion to myself has allowed me to "see" my students more clearly and to be more compassionate and kind to them, realizing that certain behaviors may have more to do with what happened in their home the night before or what they did or didn't have for breakfast that morning. I also realize that the way I react to them has more to do with me and how I'm feeling in that moment than with them!

"Inner Practices" identified the concept of "right intentions and skillful means." On a basic level, this is being present in a situation, waiting to respond, and then responding correctly. My intention was to find my voice and speak up for myself, but I had to learn how to do so, skillfully, without insult. One particular example was a colleague joking about so many of us taking this "touchy-feely" course. The colleague had, in jest, made several unsupportive comments over the time period of several weeks, starting before the course had even begun. I had let it go a few times, in spite of hearing rumblings from staff members and feeling it to be negative myself. One morning, she made yet another comment in front of me and another student from the "Inner Practices" class, and I brought it to her attention. I told her that some people were offended by her comments and that she should really be careful. After the exchange, I realized I could have handled the situation much better by speaking to her one-on-one at a time when I wasn't reacting. However, I was pleased that I spoke up. The colleague and I eventually had a conversation about it, and she now realizes that joking can sometimes come across as unsupportive. I'm still working on finding my voice—I have the right intentions, but now must work on the skillful means.

Creating "space" in the classroom was also addressed in the course as a way of showing compassion. Creating space can mean wiping the slate clean after a disciplinary incident, or it can mean allowing time for thoughtful answers. It can also mean giving students a chance to breathe—time to process information and get their creativity flowing before they start work on a project. I have always provided that space in my classroom, but it was unintentional, and I wasn't really aware of its purpose. I actually thought that the space I was creating was not a good thing—I thought the students should be constantly busy, working every second of class time. "Time on task," the administrators like to say—I've always had a problem with that. My classroom is, at times, noisy and chaotic, but it seems to work.

Now I realize that creating space is necessary. At a recent parent/teacher conference, it was evident that allowing space is a good thing. Several parents of students who were graduating told me that their children would probably not have made it through high school without my class—that the class created a place in their day to continue learning, but to learn in a relaxed atmosphere, in their own way, in their own time. One parent even said that the class provided the space (yes, space!) for her child to explore different career avenues. Recently, I got an email from a former student, who told me:

> I learned more than you think I did from you. But the cameras and computers aside, that classroom was the only place I went to every school day for three straight years and I wouldn't have made it through high school well without it. So I appreciate the sacrifices you made to make that a comfortable place for me. . . . It means a ton to me.

Wow!

On a personal level, the most important insight I've gotten is that all of this really does require practice—that I will not be a perfect teacher all of the time. Showing compassion to myself when I backslide or have a not-so-great day gets me back on track more quickly. I try to treat myself as I would a friend who is having the same issues. I still have many days when I'm feeling inadequate, when I may feel a little "off," when I might react a little too quickly. But I know deep inside that I am enough. I'm human. And so are my students.

"When we experience ourselves directly and with compassion, we begin to relax and take our place in the classroom just as we are" (Brown, 2002, p. 2). What has happened to me and what I now bring to my classroom may not be obvious on the outside, but the inside changes are apparent to me, and they have helped me settle into teaching. I really want to be a good teacher, a good role model, and to teach more than just "the subject." And I want to *love it*. I want to truly love what I do, and yes, relax into it. That's the first time I've used that word to describe how I want to teach. I'm finally beginning to relax into my teaching. Am I a good teacher? I'm working on it!

REFERENCES

Brown, R. (2002). Taming our emotions: Tibetan Buddhism and teacher education. In Miller, J., & Nakagawa, Y. (Eds.), *Nurturing our wholeness: Perspectives on spirituality in education.* 3–12. Brandon, VT: Foundation for Educational Renewal.

Glazer, S. (Ed.). (1999). *The heart of learning: Spirituality in education.* New York: J. P. Tarcher/Putnam.

O'Reilley, M. R. (1998). *Radical presence teaching as contemplative practice.* Portsmouth, NH: Boynton Cook.

Palmer, P. J. (1998). *The courage to teach: Exploring the inner landscape of the teacher's life.* San Francisco: Jossey-Bass.

11

Integrating the Spirit with Total Body Fitness

Sue Wood and Deb Higgins

As veteran teachers of a progressive high school's wellness department, we have always embraced change, recognizing the nature and needs of our population in this twenty-first century. We work at Champlain Valley Union High School (CVU) in Vermont, in a community that approved a multimillion-dollar bond in recent years to "renovate the old and reconstruct the new facility." As construction approached completion, we had a spectacular library and two fully loaded computer labs. We had a welcoming cafeteria offering a wide array of healthy choices and promoting themes such as "Eat Local," composting, and recycling.

In the new science wing, there were spacious classrooms and labs. Throughout the building, all bathrooms were designed with time-sensitive flushing systems and automatic water faucets. A new wood-chip-burning plant has allowed us the opportunity to be more cost and energy efficient.

We also had a new fitness center. However, when the space was designed, the equipment was somehow overlooked. How could a school that had spent millions of dollars ask for more money when the community had already been so generous?

As fate would have it, that's when we were introduced to the Talk About Wellness (TAW) initiative. Its goal was to help as many students as possible deepen their inner lives and, in turn, avoid unhealthy and destructive behaviors. We were asked about our willingness to expand our program by including *spirit-related* education in our existing curriculum in exchange for support in equipping the fitness center and bolstering the nutrition program. We wondered if we were getting in over our heads, but we agreed to meet to discuss this proposal. Our team was skeptical, as this new endeavor was somewhat unfamiliar.

Teachers in the Wellness Department had experience with the spirit dimension of wellness to varying degrees. Students had been exposed to a basic understanding of this dimension in personal health classes and in off-campus Sophomore Summit workshops. These efforts had proved to be worthwhile, but lacked continuity and clear intention. The TAW initiative provided direction with suggestions and guidelines, including a student interest survey about stress-reducing activities, along with the introduction of yoga and mindfulness exercises in two health classes, followed by a formal evaluation of their impact conducted by the New England Network for Child, Youth, and Family Services.

Before implementation, questions needed to be addressed: How and where should the spirit dimension of wellness fit into the existing curriculum, and what professional training was needed to prepare teachers for this next potential adventure? What tactic should be taken by teachers who have varying backgrounds, experiences, and ideas about what "spirit" means, and how would that be shared with students?

The Wellness Department, consisting of seven certified Health and Physical Educators with minimal understanding of yoga, mindfulness, and spirit-related activities, made a decision about where best to integrate this new unit. At the ninth-grade level, students learn about the Six Dimensions of Wellness in a personal health class. Students are also required to take a personal fitness class, usually completed in their sophomore year. This mandatory personal fitness course was the perfect place to implement the new unit. After all, it provided a captive audience! As a result, three of the seven teachers had the responsibility to teach the personal fitness curriculum.

To support the preliminary work, a qualified consultant worked with the wellness teachers to create a context for adding the spirit dimension to an existing unit. We teachers began our own journey to learn what we could: researching ideas about what "spirit" means, taking yoga classes, learning Pilates, and conducting personal research about mindfulness activities. Our first attempt began with a two-week unit. Then, unexpectedly, the lead teacher who had the most experience in this area was unable to teach the unit the following semester. Two inexperienced and apprehensive teachers were left on their own to face the challenge and make it work. One of them said: "Anyone committed to finding meaning and value with yoga and mindfulness will make it happen to bring such valuable and important curriculum to the kids."

Concurrently with the new program, Tobin Hart, Ph.D., psychologist, professor, author, and cofounder of the ChildSpirit Institute in Carollton, Georgia, addressed the faculty and students at CVU. TAW provided an opportunity to meet with him and others working in the field to examine the idea of a spirit-supporting framework for educators. It was then that we realized and recognized that our commitment to yoga/mindfulness was being supported by our community, superintendent, and principal.

Our principal, Sean McMannon, stated: "I am deeply committed to the integration of spirituality into adolescent learning and leadership. I believe that students are ripe for educational opportunities that encourage the blending of the heart and the mind. When we combine our emotions and our intellect we tend to find a place of balance where there is room for clarity and growth. As educational leaders it is imperative that we create structures and programs to lay this spiritual foundation for educators and students."

BELIEVING IN AND EXPANDING OUR COMMITMENT

We continued on our journey, expanding the two-week unit to three four-week sessions. Yoga postures and Pilates exercises were woven into fitness classes. For example, we began to teach the muscle groups as we taught yoga, rather than as a lecture. With the help of volunteers and colleagues from other subject areas, mindfulness activities were taught. One of the three personal fitness teachers took Aostre Johnson's graduate course "The Heart of Learning," and all three teachers presented at the state conference for health and physical educators (Vermont Association for Health, Physical Education, Recreation and Dance) in the fall of 2007. As a result, we were asked to lead an in-service training for middle and high school teachers.

Each semester, as the personal fitness class ends, our team of teachers comes together to revise and fine tune our curriculum. The Yoga and Mindfulness Unit now stands on its own. The curriculum is outlined here.

THE PROGRAM

I. Yoga and Mindfulness Unit

The personal fitness class meets every other day for one and a half hours. The following scope and sequence changes each semester as the teachers have made revisions based on prior experience, new information, and when resources may be available.

Lesson 1
Learning Outcomes: Students explore the Six Dimensions of Wellness as suggested by the National Wellness Institute, to include: intellectual, physical, social, emotional, spiritual, and occupational. Students develop and discuss their personal support networks and identify sources of stress.

1. Teacher leads a discussion about the Dimensions of Wellness. For most students, this is a review, as they were introduced to this concept in ninth-grade personal health class. Students refer to information and a model/diagram in their notebooks.
2. Teacher leads a discussion about stress: Two lists of stressors are brainstormed and written on the board: One is a list of stressors perceived by teens. The other is a list of stressors perceived by adults. Similarities and differences are compared and discussed. Personal tools for coping are explored.
3. Class views an approved DVD to demonstrate how one teen Olympic gold medalist uses yoga as part of her daily routine.
4. Class discusses, reacts, and reflects on benefits of yoga: both to mind and body. Students begin to make the connection.

Lesson 2
Learning Outcomes: Students begin to see the mind and body connections from practicing mindfulness/meditation, and students practice beginning yoga postures to reinforce self-calming and mindfulness.

1. Class views a video clip from a *CBS This Morning* show about how one school integrates meditation into daily curriculum.
2. Class discusses ways of applying mindfulness to our school setting.
3. Teacher leads yoga practice or uses an approved DVD.

Lesson 3
Learning Outcomes: Students begin to understand how mindfulness can be practiced in a variety of ways and learn simple meditative practices.

1. A guest or colleague provides a space once a week for students to be guided in mindfulness.

Lesson 4
Learning Outcomes: Students learn and practice proper breathing and stress management while practicing yoga and mindfulness activities.

1. Teacher leads or uses an approved teaching DVD on breathing.
2. Teacher leads or uses an approved teaching DVD on yoga for flexibility.

Lesson 5
Learning Outcomes: Students experience a complete yoga and meditation session.

1. Teacher uses an approved teaching DVD on yoga and meditation.

Lesson 6
Learning Outcomes: Students continue practicing yoga postures.

1. Teacher or a guest leads yoga stretches and breathing exercises.

Lesson 7
Learning Outcomes: Students experience a fast-pace "fitness" yoga.

1. Teacher leads or uses an approved DVD.

Lesson 8
Learning Outcomes: Students experience another mind-and-body connection through Pilates practice.

1. Students gain understanding about the background/history of Pilates.
2. Teacher leads the class or uses an approved DVD to practice a Pilates sequence.

Lesson 9
Learning Outcomes: Students Learning for Yoga and Mindfulness unit is assessed.

Examples of Assessment Activity Choices for Students

- Research and then teach a yoga posture or assign in partners.
- Create a mandala representing what yoga and mindfulness mean.
- Take a nature walk, collect "things in nature," and create a mandala outdoors on the grass in quiet.
- Meditate while lying together in a circle outdoors.
- Learn how to "cloud paint" for relaxation.
- Take five minutes in class to write an "uplifting note" to a parent or friend.

- Quietly go on a hunt for four-leaf clovers.
- Research, share, and discuss inspirational quotes.
- Make a "stress box" with images of stressors on the outside and activities or tools for countering stress on the inside.

Assessment Resources for Students

- DVDs (a wide variety are used and experimented with each semester; selections are careful to emphasize wellness and relaxation and avoid religious language or suggestions)
- Community members and faculty
- Student instructors
- Articles from magazines, books, and the Internet
- Yoga mats
- Motivational posters

Other Student Assessments Assigned by Teachers

- Formative assessments: Quizzes to review assigned readings
- Reflections: Verbal and written/journal entries
- Personal responsibility: Daily participation points
- Summative assessment: Written test about the basic concepts of yoga and mindfulness as they relate to wellness

II. Mind, Body, and Spirit Journal Unit

During the next unit of study in the personal fitness class, students create and make entries in a journal. It will be used for both directed entries and free writing. Their thoughts, feelings, emotions, and reflections will be captured as they discover more about their heart and spirit while experiencing yoga, Pilates, and mindfulness activities.

Instructions to the Students

1. Use any type of paper you wish. You will make about ten entries, so plan accordingly.
2. Bind the journal together with string or a staple. Be creative.
3. Create a cover page that is self-identifying, including your name.
4. Include responses to the questions assigned, as well as reflections about class activities. The journal may also be used to share inspirational self-written or found poems. This is a substitute for many of the written assignments normally completed.

Assessment

A journal grade is earned at the completion of the unit. Assessment is based on the number of entries completed, both assigned and free, as well as the depth and breadth of the entries.

Suggested Journal Entry Topic

What is yoga? What is mindfulness? What previous experience do you have with each of them? How do you think practicing both will be useful in your life as a teenager?

SAMPLE YOGA AND MINDFULNESS JOURNAL ENTRIES

The following are excerpts from some of the journals that have been created by students.

- "This yoga class really helped me relax. I have a ballet performance coming up and am really nervous about that. I was able to have some 'me' time in this class which I don't usually get. During the quiet meditations, I'm able to think about the good things that happen. I think about my kittens that are always there for me and respond with a loving look and purr; no advice and sympathy, just love. I look forward to spending more time with yoga."
- "Yoga and meditative activities have been a very useful way for me to take my mind off my problems for a few minutes. It's an effective way for me to relieve stress."
- "The yoga allows my mind to clear and be free of thought."
- "I got really tired during the Core exercises in yoga but it also was very relaxing. I am having such a busy week with baseball tryouts, confirmation and a family gathering this weekend. It was nice to simply just relax for awhile. I know it would be good for me to do yoga for a few minutes every day when my life is busy."
- "While the yoga is sometimes difficult because I'm not very flexible, it also has been relaxing and fun. I enjoy the laid-back environment in the midst of a hectic day. It has increased my flexibility and helped strengthen my inner core."
- "I really have enjoyed the meditation piece of this unit. During school, it reduces stress and gives you the time to sort out thoughts. It's just so relaxing to go to that place where it feels as though you have nothing to worry about, no bad thoughts. All the stress just rolls off your back; it's such a calming feeling. It's even better when that feeling follows me out of class!"
- "Yoga has helped me stretch out before my baseball games. I feel I could do some yoga before I go to sleep to relax my mind. I have

been feeling a little depressed these past couple of days because my uncle died a year ago this week and I started to think about him during the session."

- "Doing yoga in personal fitness class is a good thing to do almost every class! I find it very relaxing and it makes me think simple and good thoughts. It feels good to stretch my muscles and I like doing the abdominal stuff."
- "Yoga can be hard. Not always relaxing but challenging, sometimes it was tranquil. I just sat and thought. As we progressed it became rigorous and proved to be quite a good workout."
- "Personally I think yoga is kind of weird but it does strengthen and stretch my body."
- "It's nice to get back in touch with yoga. I used to do it and recently I have been so overloaded I haven't made the time. I have oboe and guitar lessons; I'm in a band; I'm in orchestra; I rock climb and I'm on the tennis team. It has been so nice to have time to meditate and put me in a better frame of mind."
- "Yoga was sometimes painful but good. It has helped me with my work out for the class. I might not look like I like it but it is good for me and that is why I go home and do it sometimes. It helps me get rid of stress and brings me back to earth. So thank you guys for this class. You are good teachers."
- "During the yoga unit, I feel like I made several mental changes. I became more aware of my body and I feel like it made me stronger mentally. I was able to let go of worries and stressors with more ease. It allowed me to take a step back and take deep breaths. Minimizing stress has allowed me to slow down and it has had physiological benefits as well such as decreased heart rate."
- "The most significant life change in this class is in self-confidence. I have moved around a lot in my past and each time a little piece/part of my confidence would be lost. Ever since this class though, I have been gaining some back. I am much more aware of my body and I am also aware that I am not as horrible and ugly as I thought. I know I can improve and change if I really want to and this class has made me strive for that positive change. With this gain of confidence, I have become much happier and have become much more motivated to do well. My mind and body connection is greater than it ever has been. And now I know that with discipline, determination and dedication, I can do anything! Thank you—I am eternally grateful to you for these life changes!"
- "Many changes occurred for me during the mind and body unit. I now do a bit of yoga and meditation daily which has had a huge impact on my overall wellness. The meditation has really made me happier and a lot less stressed. The calm and relaxed feeling has

brought me back to painting which is my major stress reliever. Because of the techniques I learned in this class I can feel less tension in my shoulders and jaw which makes my life a lot more comfortable."

- "The unit I found to be unexpectedly beneficial was the yoga/Pilates/meditation portion of the course. Before it just seemed 'new age' to me, something the celebrities did so they could appear spiritual. It was fascinating to me, especially to see how relaxing it was. This is something I probably wouldn't have done without learning its significance. Sitting around, watching TV, eating ice-cream; that's what I would be doing instead of doing a Pilates work-out. Now I want to buy my own DVD's so I can do this at home. I really have learned a lot during this semester. Sure, some of the facts may soon be forgotten, but the concepts will always be there. Life isn't only about school and work: there are many other components as well. This course has taught me to see what these components are and how to improve upon them. You cannot put a grade on that: it's something that stays with you forever."

- "The mind and body unit was one of the most thought provoking units for me. I always viewed the mind and body separate in the way that I worry about how intelligent my brain is and then I worry about how fit my body is. This unit taught me that the connection between the two is strong. A lot of what goes on in my mind, like stress, greatly affects my fitness and I didn't realize this until this unit. Knowing this, I've made changes to my stress levels and it has improved how I feel overall."

- "When I started the yoga class, I began to be more peaceful. At first I thought yoga is just a class where you put your feet on top of your neck but (I learned) it helps your emotional and physical feelings. Now I know it's much about my attitude and how I balance all six dimensions of health."

- "This class has given me the drive to really get in shape for the first time in my life and I'm ready to work for it. I am beginning to practice yoga at home and my flexibility has improved. I can finally touch my toes. . . . I've never been able to do that!"

CONCLUSION

When the students' reflective journals demonstrated increased meditative and mindfulness practices in their lives, we became energized to do more. The new program was no longer a pilot, but now an integrated part of the curriculum. Dense and hurried schedules often increase stress and pose the greatest challenge to doing more of this work in a school setting. Ironically, that is why it is needed.

12

Stress Reduction in a Middle-Level Social Studies Class

Deborah Thomsen-Taylor

As a middle school teacher, I wanted to connect with my students at a deeper level so that they could achieve at a higher level. I enrolled in a course that explored the various "capacities" that help to deepen one's learning experience. For my assignment, I chose to explore the capacity of self-calming, or stress reduction, because of challenges I had encountered in the classroom.

Rolling eyes, moans, and a few shocked faces greeted me when I told my classes we would be starting a research project. Like many middle-grades social studies teachers, a massive research paper is a yearly project in my classes. Helping students with the tasks of selecting viable topics, designing focus questions, collecting references/sources, note taking, and improving informational writing skills is part of the long, complicated affair. I believe wholeheartedly that my students need to learn how proper research is done, but it can be a very difficult month for teacher and students. The process of researching and writing is overwhelming for many middle schoolers.

"Mrs. Taylor, why do we have to do this every year?" inquired one reluctant eighth grader.

"Just wait. It will be different this year. I promise," I tried to reassure them.

"How will it be different?" asked the skeptical student.

"I have lots of ways to help you stay organized, focused, and reduce your stress," I said.

And so it began. My goal was to accompany the annual research process with a variety of modifications that would help my students in our classroom and beyond. Ideally, they would learn to use several strategies of time management and techniques for stress reduction that could also be used in other classes and in their general lives. I was very open to introducing these new concepts in the classroom. We learned about deep breathing, chair yoga, and even visualization. From my perspective, it was energizing to use these new concepts and very rewarding to see my students calm and productive.

PROJECT CHALLENGES AND SUCCESSES

In the ideal classroom, children enjoy the subject matter, challenge themselves to expand upon learning, and complete assignments on time. Reality often paints a different picture! Many middle school students struggle with feeling engaged and motivated when they don't understand exactly what is expected of them. In my experience, the more challenging the assignment, the more likely students will shut down and not complete the necessary work. My students' research project was no exception to any of these problems.

It was my goal to help students complete all sections of their projects. In looking through my grade books for the past three years, I noticed an alarming trend of late work around the research project. In one class of twenty-six students, the following components of the paper were turned in late: thirteen "pre-writes" (focus questions and note cards), fifteen first drafts, and eight final drafts. In another class of twenty-four students, the following were late: thirteen pre-writes, seven first drafts, and five final drafts. If 50 percent of the class could not complete part of this project on time, something had to change!

As educators, we recognize that compiling research takes time. Certain steps must be completed in sequence. From the teacher's standpoint, it is frustrating when classroom lessons cannot move forward because students have not completed necessary steps. I know that many teachers would agree it seems unfair (for all parties) to move into the next skill section when the previous section has not been completed by a majority of the class—but we do move on. The student who was falling behind is now even further behind, and it will be only a few days before he or she gives up completely. For my students' success and happiness, I was willing to make some big changes for this year's project.

I am fortunate to have a "looping team," so my students and I are together for four years. We get to know each other very well. One of the greatest advantages of this four-year model is that the relationship we build over those years achieves a high level of respect and trust. This year my eighth graders are adventurous. They will try something just for the sake of it. The seventh graders are a bit more reserved and tend to look to their peers to decide if something is worth trying. These observations are important to note when reflecting upon the activities I would ask my students to experience. There would be some risk, in the sense that trying something new can be met with skepticism.

My first area of focus to minimize stress and help students deal with this colossal project was time management in the form of a research handbook and a calendar of due dates. I will admit it—I am someone who thrives on organization. In some ways, having the information lined up in advance made *me* a better teacher.

The kickoff for our research project was the calendar of due dates. I like working with middle school students on organizational skill building, and providing a monthly calendar helped my students reduce some stress. I have many students who become anxious about exactly when things are due. Having tasks broken down into manageable pieces was helpful to many of them. My students are procrastinators, too. Asking for components of the project in a reasonable amount of time was helpful to them. One small baby-step toward stress reduction was done!

Here are a couple of comments I later received from students about this project:

- "I like how we broke down the deadlines for the report. If we hadn't done that, I probably would have procrastinated and saved it until a few days before it was due."
- "I liked how writing this report was really spread out also. It helped that you didn't tell us 'ok, here is what you need to do and it is due in a week.' Especially because I procrastinate a lot! It helped me to have due dates for different pieces of the project at different times. Like the note cards, then the outline, first draft, and other drafts after that."

In looking back on the grades for these seventh- and eighth-grade classes, a very small number of assignments—selecting topics, focus questions, note cards, first drafts, and so on—were considered late. In my seventh-grade class (twenty-four students), the late assignments came from one student who has a modified accommodation as part of his 504 education plan. A similar trend could be seen in the eighth-grade class (twenty-two students), where one student also has accommodations for extra time as part of his Individualized Education Program.

This year, for the most part, barring absences, very few assignments were late from either class—just two assignments out of the entire project were not completed on time. Compared to past years of teaching the research project, when almost half of the assignments were late, I consider these moves toward wellness and stress reduction a huge success. My students felt successful, and I did, too.

The next part of student stress reduction was allotting class time to complete various requirements. This may seem like a given, but, in the past, the process of researching and writing for my classes was completed as homework. This year, the entire process was to be classified as *in-class* work. I am firm in telling my students, "If I give you class time—you will use it or lose it." I was pleasantly surprised by the many class periods when I sat at the middle round table to answer questions, monitor progress, and serve as the classroom barometer, noticing who was struggling or needed extra help. My students did use class time beautifully! They lived up to my highest expectations. In my opinion, it was the combination of time management aspects, class time, and especially the addition of wellness practices that really helped make this project a success for both teacher and students.

- "Doing the report and everything mostly in class had made it SOOOO much less stressful for me. I know if it had been for homework, I would be working on it for a while and that is really stressful for me! Also, it helps to do it in class because we can ask you more questions and we get more feedback which also makes our work better! Thanks Mrs. Taylor!"
- "I think that how you gave us time to work on our report during class helped me a lot. If you did not give us time to work, I probably wouldn't have even thought to start working on my report yet."
- "This class has been less stressful because we had lots of time in class to work and took breaks often. We are also working at school so all my resources are at hand and readily available. We can also ask for help whenever we need it. Mrs. Taylor has also given us many ways to lower our stress when we are working."

WELLNESS PRACTICES

The wellness practices that I regularly incorporated into these classes were deep breathing, chair yoga, stretch breaks, and visualization activities. On several days, we also began classes with a short contemplative reflection before moving into a more traditional minilesson on research or writing strategy. My goal was to improve work quality and focus. Originally, I was hesitant to try many of these wellness strategies with my students—it is not my style. However, the wellness course offered a variety of techniques that I believed would help make my students become even better learners and young adults.

The deep-breathing techniques I introduced to my middle school students could be considered deep, cleansing breaths. As adults, we know how a few deep breaths can help us calm down at stressful times. Our students deserve to be taught this same idea—a deep breath can help them relieve tension and improve their focus. My students particularly enjoyed the "hot chocolate breathing," in which they imagined they were holding a mug of hot chocolate and inhaling its warmth and aroma. Other students, boys more than the girls, seemed to enjoy deeply inhaling through the nose, holding it for five seconds, and then exhaling slowly through the mouth.

To reiterate, my goals for this research project were for students to complete assignments on time and stay focused for class periods and to help them reduce overall stress levels. Having noticed my students' ability to stay focused for a fifteen- to twenty-minute window, I wanted to balance the forty-five minutes students had to work on their research project with time for them to stay calm and focused.

Chair yoga and simple stretch breaks helped them learn to monitor their own needs. I wanted them to physically feel the difference within their bodies after a few simple stretches. Chair yoga or getting out from behind the computers became an ingrained part of our classes after a few days. At the beginning of our research project, I taught several simple stretches they could do at their chairs. Then, when they were working, I monitored the clock and, in a quiet voice, suggested every fifteen minutes that they practice their new stretches.

After a few days, I no longer needed to suggest the stretch break; the students did them on their own. The students' level of involvement, when stretching every ten to fifteen minutes, was at least 80 percent. The overall demeanor of a class was very calm, quiet, and focused. I never would have believed these students would work hard for forty-five-plus minutes by simply self-regulating their own need for a deep breath or a stretch. I have several active students who find focusing a challenge, and even they benefited from the stretch breaks, which became known as "focus breaks."

Some days, we began with a visualization activity. This became successful when I realized how many talented athletes, dancers, musicians, and actors I have as students. We practiced by comparing visualizations of the perfect shot, pass, dance, song, or scene. Then we visualized what the perfect classroom, research, typing, or fact-finding mission would look like. Young students need comparisons when exposed to a new concept. We tried visualization several times at the start of class, and I enjoyed the tone it seemed to create for the remainder of the period. We live in a rushed world. Easing into the class and visualizing what could be accomplished was very helpful to some students.

- "The calming yourself by thinking you're breathing in a cup of soup or hot chocolate also helped. Thank you!"
- "I think that it is a little less stressful in Social Studies because you are letting us take breaks every once and a while to relieve stress. It is very helpful to me."
- "I think that much more has been done this year to help with our stress as a student. The homework is small, and what big projects we do have to do are given large amounts of class time. The stress relieving breaks and methods that we do in class also have helped."
- "A way we decreased stress was taking some time at the beginning of class to go over some aspect of the report (as we have already been doing). We do not start working immediately. Instead, the kids relax, think and adjust to Social Studies Class."
- "It's definitely helped that we've been working on them [reports] a lot during class. . . . It helps that we can go over something like note taking and then just go and use that information while we're working. I really like being able to do my work here, where I have all my resources—if I need to talk to them. [This student was interviewing teachers at our school.] I also really like the stress reducers, like the mug of hot chocolate (or pumpkin spice latte, however you want to look at it)."

A FINAL WORD

I am the type of teacher who persists with something that works and makes modifications based on my teaching style and my students' reactions, although what works for one teacher in one particular class may not work for another. Perhaps teachers develop a sixth sense of their classrooms, sensing when their students are stressed, anxious, or shutting down because they are overwhelmed with an assignment. I now know that calming myself and offering supportive strategies to my students can make a world of difference in their behavior and learning.

13

Teaching Children Empathy

Jessica Toulis

What is wrong with these young children? Why are they so disengaged? Why are they unmotivated? Aren't they supposed to be excited about learning—little sponges, always wanting more? Why are they treating each other so poorly? Why don't they have patience and understanding for one another?

I asked myself these questions daily as I entered my classroom full of third and fourth graders. As a passionate teacher who loves children, I was so disheartened and frustrated with the behavior and disengagement that I was consistently seeing in these eight-, nine-, and ten-year-olds. Sadly, there were times that year when I considered leaving the profession. That is when I knew I had to find a way to make appropriate and positive changes in my classroom.

Then one day I became involved in a conversation with a parent of one of my students. I was instantly intrigued by his perception of public education and how public schools seem to ignore the spirit dimension of the whole child. Honestly, it was something I had never taken much time to think about. We continued our conversation for quite some time, and by the end I was ready to take "Heart of Learning," a three-credit graduate course that focused on the inner spirit of the child.

This course was life changing. I learned that all I had intuitively wanted to do with children in my classroom was very appropriate. It gave me wonderful ideas to help me create a positive, stress-free, and anxiety-free classroom. I learned that movement, fun, laughter, breathing, stretching, and relaxing were just as important to the children and their success as the curriculum and standards I had been too focused on. I learned that making deep and lasting connections with children and their families provided an amazing foundation that created lifelong relationships of mutual respect and love. As a result, I had the most amazing school year and was truly saddened when it came to an end.

The final assignment for the "Heart of Learning" course was to write a unit that incorporated at least one topic we had focused on throughout the semester. Because I had been so disheartened in the past by the way children were treating one another, I chose to write a unit on teaching children empathy and teaching them to listen with understanding and empathy.

RATIONALE

The first reason I chose to focus on empathy was because I believe that it's extremely important to promote caring, kindness, and compassion for others. The second reason was because it has been a personal goal of mine to integrate the "habits of mind" into the culture of my classroom. Habits of mind are "broad, enduring, and essential lifespan learnings" whose purpose is to "help educators develop thoughtful, compassionate, and cooperative human beings who can live productively in an increasingly chaotic, complex, and information-rich world" (Costa & Kallick, 2000 xiii).

There are several habits of mind, but I chose "listening with understanding and empathy" as the first to work on with my students. Before I could teach this, however, I first needed to teach what empathy was, with the goal of providing students with the building blocks to become empathetic and compassionate people.

UNIT PLAN FOR EMPATHY

Essential Learning Outcomes

- Learn what it means to be empathetic
- Understand the importance of empathy
- Practice regularly being empathetic toward others
- Listen with understanding and empathy

Guiding Questions

- What is empathy?
- Why is it important to be empathetic toward others?
- Why is it important to listen and understand with empathy?
- How do we show empathy?
- How do we listen with understanding and empathy?

Length of Unit

- Three weeks, 30–45 minutes per day, or adapted
- Easily integrated into other subject areas, such as read aloud, etc.

UNIT ACTIVITIES FOR UNDERSTANDING EMPATHY

1. Role Model

Model empathy through compassionate words and behaviors toward students and other people in school and in life. Care for others, think about and acknowledge how they are feeling, and empathize with them.

Read aloud and discuss: Read aloud to students books that provide a good basis for discussion about how a character feels and shows empathy or that allow students to empathize with the character. Then either discuss these examples with the students as a whole group or allow them to discuss in small groups, perhaps later sharing ideas with the larger group.

Following are some good choices for children's literature that highlights empathy:

- Blume, Judy, *The Pain and the Great One* (Tate, 1984)
- Bunting, Eve, *Riding the Tiger* (Houghton Mifflin Harcourt, 2001)
- Cannon, Janell, *Stellaluna* (Houghton Mifflin Harcourt, 2007)
- Cheng, Andrea, *Grandfather Counts* (Lee & Low Books, 2003)
- Cherry, Lynne, *The Great Kapok Tree* (Harcourt Brace Jovanovich, 1990)
- Coles, Robert, *The Story of Ruby Bridges* (Scholastic Press, 2004)
- Daly, Niki, *Once Upon a Time* (Farrar, Straus & Giroux, 2003)
- Danneberg, Julie, *First Day Jitters* (Charlesbridge, 2000)
- DeRolf, Shane, *The Crayon Box That Talked* (Random House, 1997)
- DiCamillo, Kate, *The Miraculous Journey of Edward Tulane* (Candlewick Press, 2009)
- Fox, Mem, *Guillermo Jorge Manuel José/Wilfred Gordon McDonald Partridge* (San Val, 2003)
- Hiaasen, Carl, *Hoot* (Random House, 2004)

- Hiaasen, Carl, *Flush* (Random House, 2007)
- Lamorisse, Albert, *The Red Balloon* (Doubleday, 1978)
- McKissack, Patricia C., *The Honest-to-Goodness Truth* (Simon & Schuster, 2003)
- Myers, Christopher, *Wings* (Scholastic Press, 2000)
- Paterson, Katherine, *Bridge to Terebithia* (HarperCollins, 1987)
- San Souci, Robert D., *The Talking Eggs* (Penguin, 1989)
- Spier, Peter, *People* (Doubleday, 1988)
- Van West, Patricia E., *The Crab Man* (Turtle Books, 2001)
- Viorst, Judith, *Alexander and the Terrible Horrible No Good Very Bad Day* (Aladdin Paperbacks, 1987)
- Woodson, Jacqueline, *Visiting Day* (Scholastic Press, 2002)
- Zolotow, Charlotte, *William's Doll* (HarperCollins, 1985)

2. Define Empathy

After reading and discussing several books, create a chart with "Empathy" in the middle. Allow students to share their ideas on what they think empathy is (use the word *empathy* often in all previous conversations during read-alouds and discussions). Using students' ideas, come up with a developmentally appropriate definition of *empathy*. An example of this may be "Understanding how someone else feels; sharing another person's feelings." Next, have students complete the "Empathy: Looks Like, Sounds Like" chart (see table 13.1) working with a partner. After they have had time to do that, bring them back together as a group and have them share ideas to create a class.

Looks Like...	Sounds Like...

Table 13.1.

3. "Courageous Conversations"

Have students brainstorm solutions to difficult social situations. Do one or two as a class and then have students do one in a small group, later sharing their solution with the class. For example, "a boy being left out of a game at recess, or what to do if everyone seems to be picking on one kid" (Delisio, 2006; see also Levine, 2005).

4. Role-playing with the Entire Group

As a whole class, offer several scenarios that require children to think about how someone is feeling, and then ask willing volunteers to demonstrate to the class how they could react showing empathy. For example, a student is told on the playground that he or she is not welcome to join the soccer game going on during recess.

5. Role-playing in Small Groups

Organize students in small groups and ask them to create a scenario in which empathy plays a key role, then have them role-play the scenario as well as the empathetic behavior. Have students present their role-play to another small group in the class and then discuss.

6. Journal Writing

Read excerpts from literature, then have students write journal entries. They may be asked to react, from the character's perspective, on how they were feeling or be asked how the characters could behave empathetically to help make other characters in the story feel better. The literature will be varied and may be fiction or nonfiction (see book list in first unit).

7. "Event Empathy Action"

David A. Levine (2005) proposes an exercise called "Event Empathy Action" (EEA):

> The EEA is a three-step advanced listening approach that teaches students how to respond to others empathetically. The EEA method is presented to the group using empathic situations, which are hypothetical scenarios a class can discuss in order to explore various empathetic responses. The hope is that in time children will naturally respond to others with empathy after thinking through these three questions:

- What happened? (identify the event)
- How is that person feeling? (understanding the other person's feelings leads to empathy)
- What will I do? (decide on a specific action to respond to the event) (Delisio, 2006, sidebar)

Use this as a format for small- and large-group discussion and have students write responses to these three questions. Some may choose to share their written responses.

8. Empathy Project

Have each student create a project to present to the class on what it means to them to be empathetic toward others. This project should be defined and created after all of the other activities listed are complete. Give them a few ideas (see list below) and allow them, as a whole group, to brainstorm additional ideas so that students can choose how they want to represent their own learning. Here are a few suggestions as to how students can choose to represent their learning of empathy:

- Make a collage.
- Write a song.
- Write a poem.
- Create a painting or other form of artwork.
- Create and act out a television commercial.

9. Why Is Empathy Important?

Discuss this question as a class, then have students write a journal entry explaining why they believe time has been taken to learn about and discuss empathy. They should share why they believe empathy is important and give a specific example of a time that they have shown empathy or have had someone treat them empathetically, and how it made them feel.

UNIT ACTIVITIES FOR LISTENING
WITH UNDERSTANDING AND EMPATHY

1. Model, Discuss, and Practice "Whole Body Listening" with the Class

Students should listen with their entire bodies when someone is speaking. Go over eye contact as well as other body language with students. Have them practice using their whole bodies when listening to each other.

2. "The Talking Stick"

Linda Starr (2006) describes a lesson plan for introducing a "talking stick" to the class:

- Explain to students that in many Native American tribes, people used a "talking stick" to make sure that each person had a turn to share his or her ideas and opinions with the rest of the group. The person holding the stick had the right to speak. Everyone else was expected to listen with respect. When a person finished talking, he or she passed the stick to someone else.
- Have students sit in a circle and give the stick to a student who is comfortable speaking to a group. Ask that student to share something with the class. You might specify a topic or let students choose their own. When the first student finishes sharing, he or she passes the stick to the student on the right. Tell students that anyone who doesn't want to speak can simply pass the stick to the next person. Students should continue passing the stick until each person has had a chance to speak. You might want students to pass the stick more than once so some of the shyer students have a second chance to share their thoughts, but don't insist that a student talk if he or she doesn't want to.
- You can use this activity in a variety of situations, including conflicts between two students who have trouble listening to each other's point of view.

3. Active Listening Activities

Teach, model, and practice active listening skills with students. They should have many opportunities to practice active listening with each other. A great time to use this skill is during conflict resolution. Students need to practice active listening when they are in conflict with another student. One student speaks at a time, explaining his or her perspective of what happened, how it made him or her feel, and what he or she would like to change. During this, the other student listens actively, without speaking, and then responds with the same process once the first person is finished speaking.

4. Self-reflection

As students become familiar with the idea of empathy and what it means to be empathetic, have them reflect on their own empathetic behavior as well as their ability to listen with understanding and empathy (see the empathy performance checklist in table 13.2). They can do this in journal format or through drawing and should be given immediate written or verbal feedback.

Indicators: I demonstrate these behaviors...	Yes	No
Helpful Actions • Acts of Kindness		
Attentive Listening • Paraphrasing • Spending time talking		
Concerned Expressions • Head nodding in agreement • Similar emotions		
Interested Questions • "Tell me more." • "I want to understand."		
Affirming Statements • "I understand." • "I care about you." • "I want to help you."		

Table 13.2.

Even though separate, specific activities are listed, this is the type of unit that is ongoing and integrated into everything that is done throughout the entire school year. Young children need constant reminders, modeling, and discussion of what empathy is, how to be empathetic, and how to listen with understanding and empathy. Empathy is something that we want everyone to have and use throughout their lives. We want it to become a lifelong habit of mind.

UNIT ASSESSMENT

Students will demonstrate knowledge through:

- Whole-group and small-group discussions and student discourse
- Regular practice of empathetic behavior with others
- Written journal entries and other written activities
- Role-playing
- Regular listening to one another with understanding and empathy
- An empathy project
- A weekly self-reflection journal

CONCLUSION

I was able to implement the entire unit and had the following successful results.

An autistic child came into my room without friends or connections to his peers. By the end of the school year, this child was treated with the same love and respect by all of his peers as everyone else. He performed in our talent show with a classmate. The classmate had eagerly volunteered to play with him, and they sat next to one another as the two of them took turns playing a keyboard during the performance.

After this curriculum, the children in my classroom were kind and caring toward one another. They were supportive when someone was in need. They did an excellent job of sharing their own stories to help a classmate feel better and show that they knew how the classmate truly felt. A great example of this was when one student was extremely nervous about presenting a project in front of the class. A classmate who had already presented (and who had been nervous as well) talked this student through his nervousness and gave him wonderful support and positive feedback during his presentation.

Many children formed very strong connections with the others, and incredible relationships were formed. Regardless of whom they were sitting with at their table or whom they worked with in a small group, they were happy and chatty, and they took extremely good care of each other.

The class was noticed throughout the school. Art, music, and physical education teachers were excited when my students came to them. This was the most successful and gratifying school year that I had experienced. My students were remarkable individuals who truly came together as a community of learners and friends, and I have rediscovered my passion to teach.

REFERENCES

Costa, A. L., & Kallick, B. (Eds.). (2000). *Activating and engaging habits of mind.* Alexandria, VA: Association for Supervision and Curriculum Development.

Delisio, E. R. (2006). *Ways to teach empathy skills* [interview with David Levine]. Retrieved from www.educationworld.com/a_issues/chat/chat166.shtml.

Levine, D. A. (2005). *Teaching empathy: A blueprint for caring, compassion, and community.* Bloomington, IN: Solution Tree.

Starr, L. (2006). *The talking stick.* Retrieved from www.education-world.com/a_lesson/00-2/lp2063.shtml.

14

Counseling from the Heart

Madelyn Nash

When I began my career as a kindergarten teacher during the 1960s, I felt fortunate to have the flexibility to create curriculum and encourage my students' discovery by using a medley of experiences that allowed them, and me, to explore and learn in a variety of ways. We utilized movement and music (eurhythmics was becoming popular then with many early education teachers), art media of all kinds, creative play, and countless learning games that I had created with my students, all focused on whatever theme or unit we were studying.

A rich mixture of learning activities were already a part of every day before I had ever heard of Howard Gardner's "multiple intelligences." How could I work with children at this age and not have a multimodal, developmental, holistic approach? It seemed a natural way to work with students. And now, as a counselor, having taken a course at Saint Michael's College with Aostre Johnson that encourages educating from the heart, I have revisited the work of people like Parker Palmer (2003), Rachael Kessler (1998/1999), Nel Noddings (2005), and Linda Lantieri (2001) as a natural extension of my early philosophical interest in how to best engage students in learning.

My own first experience with school was dismal. I was incredibly frightened of the large building, my teacher, and everything that happened within those walls. School seemed cold, formal, scary, and the furthest thing from inviting and safe for a five-year-old. I know this early experience fostered a long-term interest in creating connections with students, as Palmer so eloquently writes about not only in "The Heart of a Teacher" (2003) but also in his earlier book *To Know as We Are Known* (1983).

I determined early on that I would not be like the distant, cold teachers I had had in kindergarten and first grade, but rather someone my students could come to know and feel safe with. My journey as a teacher and then as a counselor in the classroom has been about finding my style, as Palmer (2003) encourages us to do. Palmer reaffirms for me that there is no one way to be a good teacher, but rather a way each of us finds to share our true self, our enthusiasm for our subject matter, and our willingness to be vulnerable.

MAKING CONNECTIONS

I resonate with Palmer's (2003) notions of teaching as "weaving a web of connectedness" (p. 71) with my students, of striving to engage my students' hearts in their learning, of attending to my own inner voice and the vulnerability that is a part of good teaching. I have learned on this journey that when my students engage emotionally (with their "hearts"), they are more apt to make connections, be more self-aware, and learn. I believe as Palmer does that "[to] educate is to guide students on an inner journey toward more truthful ways of seeing and being in the world" (p. 75).

When I read authors like Palmer, Kessler, Lantieri, and Johnson (1998/1999), I say a quiet "Yes!" inside, because they understand and seek a similar path. I was given the gift of hearing Kessler speak several years ago and then working with her and our elementary school staff. She affirmed the need to quiet ourselves and give our students a moment of silence in the classroom. This seems hard to do when you see students for only about forty-five minutes per week, and sometimes not even throughout the year.

Kessler (1998/1999) helps me to see that giving students moments of silence allows them to raise the questions that are so important to them and gives them the opportunity to reflect on the topic as well as on how they feel. She reminds me that initiation and ritual are good ways to connect with students. I agree that

> students who feel deeply connected don't need danger to feel fully alive. They don't need guns to feel powerful. They don't want to hurt others or themselves. Out of connection grows compassion and passion—passion for people, for students' goals and dreams, for life itself. (p. 4)

Kessler understands and writes simply about the need all students have to belong. I value and strive to encourage this through my work with the Responsive Classroom Program and school-wide morning meetings. I also support our fifth graders doing community service and younger students adopting book buddies from a lower grade level. My lunch groups and problem solving with students are other ways that students can feel a sense of connection.

Another author we read during the "Heart of Learning" course, Lantieri (2001), has been a huge support for my work in conflict resolution. Her Resolving Conflict Creatively Program was the early foundation for the peer mediation program I established almost twenty-five years ago at a rural elementary school in northwestern Vermont. Lantieri, too, is an inspiring facilitator with whom I worked many years ago as part of a middle school conference at Saint Michael's College (Vermont) and more recently as a participant in an inner resilience pilot program. Her recognition that all children have the same need for love, purpose, tolerance, compassion, and a sense of connectedness to others and the natural world is something that I hear when I talk to parents, teachers, and children.

Lantieri and others I read during the course hold a vision that values the emotional and spiritual dimensions of children. And she encourages those of us in the field to "translate our vision into concrete steps and . . . implement it" (Lantieri, 2001, p. 12).

KEEPING THE VISION ALIVE

Making this vision present amidst the increasing movement for more testing and assessment is vital, lest it get lost in the clamor for increasing students' test scores but not their compassion and overall wellness. Without this vision, our students miss the opportunity to realize important aspects of their selves—aspects that will allow them to play a critical role in their future and that of our world. How will they do that if we lose the voices that help us understand how important it is to foster the spirit dimension of students' lives? It is people like Johnson, Lantieri, Kessler, and others who help nurture this vision and keep it alive in my work. When I do, I am more likely to help students thrive at a deeper level and, as a result, support their learning, self-awareness, connectedness, and resilience.

QUIETING ANXIETY—FOSTERING MINDFULNESS

There is a need to reach the ever-growing numbers of students who suffer from heightened anxiety since it so obviously impedes their learning.

Making the emotional and spiritual dimension of learning a priority is a natural fit in my work as a school counselor. Daniel Goleman's *Emotional Intelligence* (1995) has made us aware of the important relationship between the brain's emotional and executive functions.

In the introduction to Lantieri's book *Building Emotional Intelligence* (2008, 3), Goleman states:

> (SEL) students [who had social and emotional learning within their curriculum] not only mastered abilities like calming down and getting along better, but they also learned more effectively, their grades improved, and their test scores on academic achievement tests were a hefty fourteen percentile points higher than similar students who were not given such social and emotional learning programs.

Lantieri (2008, 17) elaborates: "Each day in my work it becomes increasingly obvious that chronic anxiety, anger, or upset feelings are intruding on children's thoughts, [and there is] less room . . . available in [their] working memory to process what they are trying to learn" (p. 17).

Despite our school's and our district's commitment to the Responsive Classroom model, it is still a struggle to provide the kind of calm learning environment that will maximize learning for all children. The Responsive Classroom values community, sharing on a personal level, and self-directed learning. The authors I read for this class affirm the need to go further by including time for reflection and ritual in my work. Instinctively, I recognize the value of both—quieting my mind makes *my* work more thoughtful and *my* interactions more focused; creating rituals with my students deepens *their* experience of an activity and its learning potential, for them as well as for me.

So, it makes sense to practice mindfulness, as Patricia Leigh Brown (2007) writes, as a way to lessen students' negative internal chatter. I want to optimize the benefits of mindfulness and moments of silence and reflection in my work with students. I want to help them use the strategies we use in guidance class during the rest of their day. I want to help them see the benefits that result as they learn to calm their thinking, lower their level of stress by simply breathing, and reflect on decisions they make that might alter their negative perspective on a situation.

As a school counselor, I often meet with students to problem-solve and invariably try to help them perceive the choices they have in their lives. For example, they can choose to calm their anxiety by practicing deep breathing. They can remove obstacles to joy by choosing a positive attitude toward a situation. They can choose to do nothing about a problem until the best choice becomes clearer. Each decision gives them a sense of their own power and encourages them to use the strategy of mindfulness and self-reflection.

SELF-REFLECTION AND MODELING

The benefits become more obvious as I become more self-reflective in my work with students. If mindfulness increases *my* insight and I model that in class or in individual sessions, perhaps my students will be more likely to employ these self-reflective practices. I see clearly in my own work and that of my colleagues the truth in the maxim "We teach best what we model." For years, I have been telling adults in my conflict resolution and mediation training, "You can't really teach about resolving conflict until you understand your own style of conflict and the way you might be modeling it in your classroom."

It is clear that until I take the time to be more reflective, practice mindfulness, use calm breathing strategies when *I* am stressed, and reflect on *my own* choices so that I can remove the self-inflicted impediments to a joyful experience of life, I will be less successful in helping my students do the same. Resisting the urge to dash from one important activity to another would also set a calmer tone. Weekly course meetings give me the opportunity to practice these strategies, reflect on my work, and keep the questions about my own practice present in a daily way. When I do this, I am more likely to create the kinds of experiences with my students that will bring positive results.

My fifth-grade unit becomes more probing as I include many of the ideas I have been practicing and discussing with other educators and counselors. Because of this class, I explore in a deeper way with my fifth graders topics such as who they are, what is important to them, and how their values affect the choices they make using a variety of artistic, reflective, and community-building rituals. I also give them the opportunity to engage in some challenges that help them to see the role they play in a group. As the unit unfolds, so does their awareness of who they are, what they think, and how they express it. The following are examples of unit activities:

- *Activity One:* Ask each student to bring in and share with others a valued object that reflects something significant about him- or herself.
- *Activity Two:* Building upon the first class, ask the students to quiet themselves with eyes closed and think about who they are, how they spend their time, and what is important to them. Then give each child a "think sheet" on which to record his individual reflections. Finally, have them choose pipe cleaners of three different colors to create a sculpture that portrays three aspects of themselves. (Prompts might include: What makes me smile? What can't I live without?)
- *Activity Three:* A new reflection sheet is called "All About My Family," and the students are asked to ponder, perhaps with a partner,

their family's country of origin, traditions, celebrations, foods, and so forth. Then a nine-block square can be illustrated on paper (or eventually on cloth) to create a personal "quilt" that ultimately joins others to represent the diversity of their class. Such an activity offers many opportunities to express various intelligences: linguistic, visual, inner- and intrapersonal, and kinesthetic.

HELPING STUDENTS FIND THEIR VOICES

So often in education, we think about academic results without thinking about the other ways in which a child needs to be nurtured. Johnson's (1992) words resonate: "The recognition of qualitative thinking is nurtured by a sense of relaxation and unhurried time" (p. 33). If qualitative thinking, based in feeling-intuition, is really the precursor to quantitative thought—the soul or heart of thinking—then I can look for better ways to slow down the process, the pace of the class, and help students rediscover the depth of thought that can flourish in planned moments of silence. If I want to help my students find their own voice, I must allow them the quiet in which to hear it.

In education, there are many voices that intrude on our work and insist on more and more "district initiatives" that take away that sense of relaxation and unhurried time in our day. I seek to find a more relaxed pace with my students. I want them to know that I value their thoughts, that their voices matter, and their responses become more thoughtful as a result. The quieter students who need more time to pull their thoughts together are valued. Those who seek the "first response" position are invited to take time to review their thoughts and give others the chance to be heard first.

PRACTICING MINDFULNESS NOW AND IN MY WORK

The format of courses such as "Heart of Learning: Exploring the Depth of Education" allows me to play with ideas and then take time between class sessions to practice how best to implement some of them. During one of our classes led by Dr. Aostre Johnson, Richard Brown was invited to visit. He spoke about bringing the practice of observation, meditation, contemplation, and compassion to our teaching. His words remind me that teaching is an important part of what brings meaning to my life. Sometimes when my schedule gets crowded with student meetings, parent encounters, and teacher concerns about a child, I become preoccupied with reviewing or making mental notes on these needs when I prefer to be focused on what Brown (1998/1999) refers to as the "sacredness of everyday learning."

It is that feeling of the preciousness of the moment that I value, and ironically it is when I am not trying so hard that it happens most. When I am feeling relaxed and in tune with the students and the teacher whose class I am visiting, my mind (or perhaps my heart) works better. I remember students' names with no difficulty, despite the 140 new students on my caseload. I feel comfortable letting the teaching process unfold instead of thinking beyond where we are at that moment in class. I am more comfortable with who I am and less "in my head," more aware of "seeing" and less focused on "looking" for some particular response (Brown, 1998/1999, p. 2). I also experience no anxiety because, as Brown told us, I am not stuck in some abstraction that doesn't reflect the present experience.

I am reminded during this class that mindfulness takes patience and practice. When I utilize some of the centering, relaxation responses myself and apply them to my teaching, it helps both me and my students relax and be more open to learning from the class experience. I plan to try many of the ideas from "Please Help Me" (Boyce, 2007) with my students, perhaps as a beginning to a class or as a closing reflection, to give students and myself the opportunity to practice being more present. When I practice mindfulness, I model for my students that I value it and use it myself.

ACHIEVING MY PURPOSE

If I want my work to achieve its purpose—to be meaningful for my students—I have to recognize, as Lantieri (2001) does, that many years of teaching students the skills of conflict resolution, impulse control, and reading and identifying feelings will not get us where we want to go with them. If we want students to truly incorporate mindfulness and have a sense of spiritual connection, we need to nurture their inner lives.

There are many ways in which to encourage this: morning meetings, helping students to feel safe by being accepting and supportive, building in time for silence and reflection. I can value all of their voices when processing in class and encourage a variety of ways for students to express their particular strengths. I can become more aware of what is going on in my own body and mind during class and encourage my students to tune into their own bodies and minds to help them discover what they think and feel. Doing so helps them to independently discover what they have to say. These are ways I can educate from the heart.

When educating from the heart, I ask myself the same questions I ask of my students: What is working? What was my role? How did it help the group? What might I do differently next time? I seek a colleague's support when I need it. I invite a friend to attend an exciting workshop or class that I know will rejuvenate me. I talk about this vision for education with others who will keep our enthusiasm for this work alive and growing. All of this is a work in progress.

Each successful or thoughtful interchange with my students helps them to develop a dimension of themselves that they may not have valued before. And if I achieve the vision of nurturing the emotional and spiritual lives of my students, they will discover and appreciate their own voices, their sense of purpose, and resilience—a gift for them and for me.

REFERENCES

Boyce, B. (2007, January). Please help me. *Shambala Sun, 66*–73, 119.

Brown, P. L. (2007, June 12). In the classroom, a new focus on quieting the mind. *New York Times.* Retrieved from www.nytimes.com/2007/06/16/us/16mindful.html.

Brown, R. C. (1998/1999). The teacher as contemplative observer. *Educational Leadership, 56*(4), 70–73.

Goleman, D. (1995). *Emotional intelligence: Why it can matter more than IQ.* New York: Bantam.

Johnson, A. N. (1992). The development of creative thinking in childhood. *Holistic Education Review, 5*(2), 25–33.

———. (1998/1999). Many ways of understanding and educating spirit. *Classroom Leadership, 2*(4), 1–5.

Kessler, R. (1998/1999). Nourishing students in secular schools. *Educational Leadership, 56*(4), 1–5.

Lantieri, L. (Ed.). (2001). *Schools with spirit: Nurturing the inner lives of children and teachers.* Boston: Beacon.

———. (2008). *Building emotional intelligence: Techniques to cultivate inner strength in children.* Boulder, CO: Sounds True.

Noddings, N. (2005). What does it mean to educate the whole child? *Educational Leadership, 63*(1), 8–13.

Palmer, P. (1983). *To know as we are known: A spirituality of education.* San Francisco: Harper & Row.

———. (2003). The heart of a teacher. In Ornstein, A. C., Behar-Horenstein, L. S., & Pajak, E. F. (Eds.), *Contemporary issues in curriculum* (pp. 66–76). Boston: Allyn & Bacon.

15

Nurturing Children's Inner Resources: An Elementary School Guide

Auriel Gray

As a child who moved frequently, I often found myself in circumstances where I needed to rely on myself for friendship and comfort. Over time and out of necessity, I learned to go inward to find strength and faith in my own capacity to face life's challenges. I learned, for instance, that in times of need, I could conjure in my mind the vivid image of a deep well containing within it an endless abundance of life-giving water. This image became a kind of personal icon. It has been an accessible and powerful reminder for me that no matter how afraid, sad, or lonely I might feel, I am always connected to a limitless wellspring.

Since discovering this visceral connection at a young age, I have felt called to work with children in a way that nurtures this precious relationship with their own inner life. Becoming a school counselor meant that I would be in the position to participate in the development of children's inner resources and their tools for accessing them. In my counseling work, however, I found that the guidance-related programs typically developed for schools primarily addressed basic social skills such as communication, self-control, and conflict resolution. While these are all important for relationship and community building, they were not entirely what inspired my initial interest in counseling children. The deeper foundational skills of reflection, self-awareness, and peaceful centeredness I believe are the most essential to my work as school counselor.

PROGRAMS AND APPROACHES THAT NURTURE SOCIAL AND EMOTIONAL LEARNING AND THE INNER LIFE OF CHILDREN

Two of the research-based curricula that my own school district has adopted, Skills for Growing (Lions Quest, 2011) and Second Step: Violence Prevention (Committee for Children, 2010), promote reflection as the first step toward impulse control and conflict resolution—that is, "stop and think." What I found in teaching the programs according to the outlined sequence was that, while most children learned to articulate the problem-solving steps, many were often unable to transfer and apply the critical first "stop and think" step in those challenging situations where they most needed to calm themselves before they could effectively move through the problem-resolution process.

It became clear to me that more emphasis and practice was needed around this initial stop-and-think step—which is essentially what Dr. Herbert Benson first described as the "relaxation response," a consciously developed reflex to counter the flight-or-fight tendency in individuals reacting to stress. This self-calming skill is grounded in the fundamental ability to counter fear with a sense of faith and trust in oneself and one's capacity to effectively meet the challenges of life.

The first guidance program I used with elementary students, Pumsy, was a social and emotional learning (SEL) education curriculum that centers on a story about a dragon named Pumsy who tries to maintain a clear mind by taking deep breaths and telling herself, "I can handle this." While the concept of trusting in one's inner resources is an important message for children, as with the other guidance programs, I found that the process of rehearsing the positive self-talk and other problem-solving steps was not enough in itself for children to anchor and access that reassuring connection with their inner resources when they most needed it.

While many guidance programs address self-awareness and reflection, they often do not focus enough on ways to build that basic sense of deep self-trust, inner resourcefulness, and spiritual connectedness from which true resiliency emerges. Many SEL curricula seem to place more emphasis on the secondary social skills, such as feelings identification and expression—which, to be effectively applied, first require developing a clear mind and calm sense of self. Increasingly I found myself wondering *how* we can best teach children to access this clear mind or state of inner peace. I began to draw from the mind-and-body practices that work best for me personally, which include a combination of movement (gentle yoga and mindful exercise), breath work, and rest (pacing and quiet).

When I was a teen, my mother, who was an enthusiastic yoga practitioner in her youth, encouraged me to take a weekly yoga class. I left the class each week with a deepened sense of peace and inner security that stayed with me between sessions and gave me a steadiness that helped to counterbalance the bumps, upsets, and mood swings typical of adolescence. I found the regular practice of gentle yoga to be a powerful means of accessing a sense of being centered and a feeling of being held or supported by a source of energy larger and more stable than my passing emotions and tenuous sense of identity. At fifteen, this yoga class was formative and life altering; it planted the seeds for a lifelong ability to cultivate a nurturing relationship, through mind-body awareness and practices, with my inner self.

As my confidence in my role as school counselor grew, I began to integrate more of my own inner-peace practices into my work with students. I wove brief relaxation-training, breath-work, and imagery exercises into my classroom lessons and group work and increasingly found that the students were not only very receptive to the mind-body practices, but would even ask for more. "When can we have another resting group?" they'd ask when they saw me after a relaxation class. I also found that students from small groups that had been introduced to yogic self-calming activities, such as the yoga pose called the "child's position," would ask if they could demonstrate poses to the class that they use for self-calming at home.

Once, a particularly volatile fifth grader spontaneously came to the front of the class to show her classmates how she used the child's position to comfort herself when she felt upset with her family. Another time, after a relaxation exercise focused on deep listening, a kindergarten student shared with the group that when she felt lonely at night she listened to the sound of her heart beating and remembered she was not alone. I was moved by how the simple yet ancient practices were transferring to the students' daily lives, as they had in my own, and was encouraged to continue integrating these holistic wellness practices in my teaching.

Another lesson I learned as a school counselor was how much we actually teach by the quality of our presence, as opposed to formal lesson content. Current findings in brain and learning research describe the function of mirror neurons in creating new neural pathways that are activated when observing the behavior and expressions of others (Iacoboni, 2008; Ramachandran, 2000).

When I began my role as a new school counselor, I soon became over-extended, trying to meet all the needs that came to my attention. I was teaching in too many classrooms and running too many groups at once. As a result, I constantly rushed from one activity to another. The counterproductiveness of this approach was illuminated to me by the candid words of a second grader who, as I arrived for one of our friendship groups, asked me, "Miss Gray, why are you always out of breath?" That was a startling reality check for me. What was I teaching my students by rushing around to such an extent? Certainly not what I wanted to be teaching them—in fact, it was in direct contradiction to the message I was trying to convey, which was the importance of knowing how to access calm centeredness.

As a result, I began to consciously slow down at work and pay more attention to finding a balance between meeting immediate needs and doing sustainable, quality work. I discovered that by tuning into my own pacing needs and adjusting my schedule accordingly, I could be more effectively present with students as well as adults with whom I interacted. Modeling the qualities of balance, calmness, and presence that I was trying to teach became a clearer priority. I found that even when I was feeling tired or overwhelmed, if I could focus my energy in the moment, as if I had all the time in the world, I could maximize the quality of attention that I brought to each person and task and thereby teach the needed self-care skills by example.

The more I bring of myself and that which moves me into my work with students, the more it nourishes me in turn. I often leave a guidance class or group in which we've done mind-body-spirit work with a renewed sense of energy, peace, and joy. Teachers have shared that they, too, look forward to the self-regulation classes that we do together for the same reason: they feel more peaceful and energized afterward.

Purely curriculum-based, didactic approaches can become redundant and tiresome, but when holistic wellness practices are integrated into developmental guidance teaching, the two combine in inspiring and energizing ways. When we spend mutually nurturing quiet time together, a collective recharge happens in that space of being calm and present with one another that becomes a welcome break from the usual busy performing mode.

Slowing and quieting down together seems to be the much-needed antidote to the busyness of our Western lives and increasing academic pressures of school. We call our brief group relaxations "minivacations," and that is indeed the function they serve. Plugging into our source, or drawing from our inner well, is a sustaining practice and vital life skill. I feel privileged to be in the position to help foster it in our students.

ACTIVITIES AND RESOURCES

The following are examples of the kinds of activities and resources I have used to support teaching self-regulation skills to elementary school students. They fall into the categories of children's stories/literature, exercise manuals, and professionally developed programs.

The general outline I follow for teaching self-regulation classes includes:

- Check-in and review of the prior week, eliciting student examples of how they have been using the wellness practices in their daily life at home and school
- Introduction of a new self-calming skill through an exercise practiced together
- A short story related to the topic of self-care and empathy
- A relaxation activity

The order of these activities may vary, but I generally end the class or group with a brief relaxation, which allows the lesson we have shared to sink in and provides a means of transitioning to the rest of the day.

Numerous children's books are suitable for teaching self-regulation skills. In selecting resources that are lesson appropriate, I follow this sequence:

1. Books and activities that address feelings and self-awareness—tuning into one's own thoughts and feelings, needs, strengths, and experience
2. Books on the topic of exploring and developing personal resources to access in response to challenges, including self-care, self-expression, and feelings/stress management
3. Resources for cultivating empathy skills

This sequence of topics follows one of my district's adopted guidance curricula, Second Step, which is typical of many developmental guidance programs. The primary difference between the Second Step model and the approach I have adapted is the integration of topical children's literature with self-regulation practices that support each skill being taught, from self-awareness to self-control and empathy.

The children's books I use with primary grades are listed at the end of this chapter under each of these topics. The challenge in fitting them into a forty-five-minute lesson has been to find relevant age-appropriate stories that are short enough to allow some remaining time for discussion. They generally take about twenty minutes or less to read. Since this timing may vary, I adjust the length of the preceding or following activity accordingly.

A favorite resource for middle- and older-grade elementary students (grades two to five) that addresses the topics of friendship and empathy is the Jataka Tales, based on Indian teaching/folk tales with animal characters. The stories are provided on CDs along with the book, and children enjoy listening to them during the relaxation part of class. Once we've entered into relaxation after a guided floor and breathing exercise and they are lying down quietly, the students are usually in a receptive listening mode. The universal core values contained in the narrated stories, such as kindness and respect, are a natural complement to their open state and are easily absorbed.

These are somewhat more abstract and sophisticated than the stories I use with kindergarten and first-grade students, although young children are also engaged by stories that use animals to teach intra- and interpersonal skills. Kindergarten teachers have told me that they will often refer back to the animal characters we've read about in class as self-regulation reminders to their students, for example, to "move more slowly like the sloth" (Carle, 2002).

I have recently come across a set of beautifully illustrated stories for younger students based on the life of Henry Thoreau that focus on presence of mind, nature, and empathy, called *Henry Builds a Cabin*, *Henry Hikes a Mountain,* and *Henry Goes to Work* (Johnson, 2002, 2003, 2006). The character of Henry in the stories is depicted as a friendly dog. The lessons in each story are very much in keeping with developing mindful self-awareness and self-regulation skills. The more one looks, the more one can find fitting, quality children's literature along these lines.

Another type of resource I have found very useful in teaching self-regulation skills is the myriad of children's yoga-oriented teachers' manuals containing many activities and games that can be easily integrated into lessons on self-awareness and self-regulation/self-care. These generally begin with various methods for teaching children breath awareness and control, which is at the core of relaxation training and focusing practices.

The manuals include simple stretches taught in conjunction with breath work, which enhance focus and balance. The stretching exercises promote self-awareness and are a precursor to relaxation, as they teach children how to notice where they are holding tension and how to release it. Since children tend to be physically oriented early in life, they naturally enjoy these grounding physical activities. Through them, they are easily motivated to learn self-regulation skills. With repeated practice in pairing their breath with calming movement, children strengthen their neurological pathways responsible for the relaxation response and thereby their capacity to access those self-calming skills more readily when they most need them.

The bibliography for this chapter contains a list of videos that I have also used for such teaching, especially with small groups. A caveat for using yoga resources in a public school is to be mindful of aspects that can be viewed as religious, such as postures that include holding hands in a prayer position. In such cases, I either skip over those parts or provide an alternative choice, perhaps a hand to the heart, folded arms, or hugging oneself. Also important is to ensure that any sounding is also neutral, such as simply humming on the out-breath as a form of breath control/extension and focus.

An excellent resource for use with groups and classes is the ALERT program *"How Does Your Engine Run?"* (Williams & Shellenberger, 1996). This is a self-regulation program developed by physical and occupational therapists for teaching children sensory integration strategies. It comes with an excellent CD that has a number of short exercises set to music to guide children through different energy states—high, medium ("just right for learning"), and low. With consciously practiced pacing and moving at various levels of energy, children learn how to notice and adjust their energy to suit the demands of a particular situation or environment.

Recent brain research has underscored the relationship between stress management and learning, and we know that a brain flooded with stress-related chemicals has difficulty retrieving and absorbing information. The ALERT manual describes exercises that target different muscle groups and major joints and are designed to provide specific sensory input affecting the brain's alertness, priming it for learning.

The program suggests using language children can identify with, such as storybook characters like Winnie the Pooh, Tigger, and Eeyore, to describe energy states they notice in themselves at different times. ALERT exercises provide the means for adjusting those states, whether in energizing or quieting ways. Children tend to respond well to the embodied simplicity of this program, and I have used it with success in kindergarten through second-grade classes.

We can teach this important fact to children: that in order to think clearly, learn, and make positive choices, they need to know how to calm their mind. Synchronizing their breath and body with their attention and imagination, they can master these processes for themselves. Since school tends to be such a cognitively oriented environment, it is no surprise that children crave activities that allow them to reconnect with their physical selves. It's a welcome lesson to learn that the brain and body are at their best when working together.

I like to introduce and integrate the ALERT exercises using related children's stories so they can see the universal applicability of the self-regulation concepts. For example, the book *Grumpy Bird* (Tankard, 2007) tells the story of a bird that got up on the wrong side of his nest, so to speak. He stomps around while different curious animal friends join and imitate him along the way, until he realizes he is beginning to have fun playing with them and his mood subsequently changes. We act out the story, stomping, hopping, jumping, and so on—all aspects of ALERT program sensory input exercises—and when we sit down afterward, we share how much fun we had and what we learned about changing our mood and mind along with our energy state.

Teachers can playfully refer back to the Grumpy Bird character when giving feedback to a child who may seem to be stuck in a low-energy state. Having enacted the story, the child is more likely to remember the energy shift in the story and, correspondingly, in himself or herself, and will thus be able to reconnect with this capacity to self-regulate more easily in the future.

Another current finding of brain research is the importance of repetition to learning (forging and strengthening new neurological pathways). The mind-body activities in the ALERT program, as well as in yoga manuals and the CD that accompanies Linda Lantieri's book *Building Emotional Intelligence: Techniques to Cultivate Inner Strength in Children* (2008), are all easily taught and practiced within brief periods of time and therefore lend themselves well to repetition.

The Inner Resilience Program's curriculum and CD are particularly useful in this regard, since they are essentially easy to use and school ready. The program is built on evidence-based practices and is designed for parents as well as teachers to use when teaching basic relaxation and focusing skills to children. The brief exercises on the CD are organized according to developmental levels and have been developed and tested for the classroom setting. They include focusing the mind (using the breath as an anchor) and relaxing the body (basic progressive muscle relaxation). The exercises can be done in short periods (five to ten minutes) and are easily integrated into each school day as a means of pacing and incorporating quiet relaxation time for both teacher and student to recharge. As an addendum to this chapter, I have included an overview of our school district's experience with piloting this innovative contemplative education program.

There are a number of children's books that complement the exercises in Lantieri's CD, such as Byrd Baylor and Peter Parnall's *The Other Way to Listen* (1978), which reinforces the listening activity and tells a story of a girl who learns to notice the sounds around her, along with the feelings within her. Lantieri includes lists of children's books in *Building Emotional Intelligence* that support the program skills. Since children naturally tend to enjoy the nurturing quality of being read to, related children's books are a valuable way to reinforce mind-body lessons and key self-regulation concepts, while also functioning as a vehicle that promotes relaxation.

Two books I've found effective for teaching about managing moods and changing emotions are *That's Good, That's Bad* (Cuyler, 1991) and

Fortunately (Charlip, 1993). Both books address the concept of life being full of ups and downs and unavoidably changing circumstances. They promote discussion of ways to stay calm and centered in the midst of things happening that often feel out of one's control.

I associate the analogy of a boat in a storm and how to safely take down one's sails, settle, and anchor, while waiting for better weather or conditions. Children in grades K–2 seem to relate readily to both stories and easily make the connection between "anchoring" and practicing slow, focused breathing (while using the senses to focus on a sound, object, nature scene, or body sensation) and balancing poses such as "the tree" (standing on one leg) to help center themselves.

ADULT SELF-CARE AND MODELING

In teaching self-trust and the value of listening to one's inner voice, it's important to model the concepts. Last spring, I was inspired to cut, from a printed chenille fabric, butterfly shapes, which I gave to individual students as part of a relaxation exercise we'd done that year. I considered these soft pieces of fabric to be transitional objects and symbolic anchors that students could take with them as reminders of their calm inner state. I anticipated that this might be more useful or meaningful for some than for others, but I took the chance even though I could see that some teachers were dubious.

This fall, a parent of a particularly anxious child called to tell me that her daughter kept the furry butterfly with her on a regular basis to help her feel calmer in stressful situations. The girl held the butterfly during a storm, for example. This spontaneous feedback affirmed for me the value of listening to my inner voice and following my own creative instincts as a counselor.

As educators whose own inner resources are vital to our efficacy, we need to continually nourish our inner lives. In the addendum, I describe two wellness programs for school staff that are essential toward this end. In particular, providing nonthreatening, secular opportunities for staff to learn and practice mind-body approaches can go a long way toward nurturing peace in the classroom and school.

When teachers feel cared for, they are better able to care for their students. The same is true for parents. With the current well-publicized findings on the importance of stress-management and attention skills to learning, and with mind-body practices such as yoga and meditation becoming more mainstream, increasing resources are available for building resilience in ourselves and our children. A "felt sense" of centeredness also provides an anchor that teachers can refer students back to at other times, saying for instance, "Let's take a slow, deep, relaxing breath and get ready to learn." Reminding students of their ability to self-regulate in this way is empowering, and it nurtures a belief in their personal capacity for self-awareness and control.

ADDENDUM: AN OVERVIEW OF THE PROCESS OF INTEGRATING THE INNER RESILIENCE PROGRAM

Over a number of years, our school district in South Burlington, Vermont, has systematically implemented the Responsive Classroom program (Northeast Foundation for Children, 2010) with most teachers having been trained in it at the elementary level, while the middle and high schools gradually implemented the corresponding affective education programs at their levels. In 2008, the district guidance team intentionally discussed ways to promote and support the continued implementation of existing affective education/wellness initiatives across the district, as we had noted an ongoing increase in levels of anxiety and stress in families and staff since 9/11. We all knew it was important to reduce further demands on already overwhelmed teachers and staff.

That same spring, a colleague shared with me an article from the *Shambala Sun* magazine entitled "Please Help Me Learn Who I Am," which described Linda Lantieri's Inner Resilience Program (IRP) being piloted in New York City schools in response to 9/11 and the resulting stress in staff and students.

We read the article as a guidance team, collectively agreed the program looked like a good fit for our purposes, and decided to look into inviting the program director, Lantieri, to our district to conduct training with staff students and parents. Toward that end, and at the timely invitation of my friend, Saint Michael's College professor of education Aostre Johnson, I attended a Spirituality and Education Network International Summit (SEN) at which Lantieri presented during the spring of 2008.

Serendipitously, Marilyn Neagley—coordinator of Talk About Wellness (TAW), a Vermont-based initiative dedicated to promoting "spirit in education"—was also at the SEN conference and was interested in bringing Lantieri and IRP to Vermont schools. With a generous grant from TAW and the support of our administration, our school district was able to offer our staff a pilot training program the following school year, 2008–2009.

We first offered interested staff a spring 2008 day of program introduction with Lantieri. Most of those participants subsequently chose to sign up for the yearlong training and implementation beginning that fall. Forty-one K–12 staff from among all five district schools participated in the first year of the IRP pilot. The program included two and a half fall training days that covered nurturing the inner life/self-care, an IRP curriculum training day, and a half-day coaching/lesson demo at each grade cluster; a two-day spring retreat focused on staff self-care and reflection; monthly ninety-minute support and practice sessions; and weekly holistic health activities offered to all staff after school.

Teacher participation and feedback was consistently strong and positive. Participants regularly expressed how much the ongoing focus and support for self-care had a healthy impact on their own lives and stress levels, including their relationships with students and colleagues. In particular, they reported that the mindfulness practices reinforced the importance of being more present in many areas of their lives and that, as a result, they had experienced an increased sense of empowerment, effectiveness, and meaning in their work.

These feelings seemed to transfer into the climate of their classrooms, where many participating teachers reported feeling better able to respond calmly to students and create a peaceful class environment. I believe an important message the teachers were getting was that their own well-being mattered—that they were cared about as human beings with their own needs. This translated into an increased capacity for them to respond effectively to the needs in their classroom.

The degree of classroom implementation varied according to teacher comfort level with the stress-reduction practices, which included basic exercises in relaxing the body and focusing the mind and were conveniently available as five- to twelve-minute guided activities on the CD that accompanies Lantieri's book *Building Emotional Intelligence* (2008). The emphasis for the first year of the pilot was on teacher self-care and familiarity with application of the contemplative practices so they could in turn comfortably model them in the classroom.

Teachers in the five third- and fourth-grade test classes, which were selected for pre- and post-program evaluation, committed to using the brief CD exercises at least every other day, with the goal being some kind of structured quiet time in class every day. The New England Network for Child, Youth, and Family Services (NEN) conducted the program evaluation, including pre- and post-tests of all staff participants, and we received preliminary outcomes in the summer of 2009.

Guidance counselors supported the program's implementation by integrating IRP-related activities into their regular guidance lessons. This generally included a children's book on a related topic (paying careful attention, using the senses/imagination to focus, finding ways to be calm, self-awareness, etc.). The book would introduce the theme and provide a jumping-off point for conversation leading into a planned activity, which gave students the opportunity to practice focusing and relaxing in different ways.

One valuable element we learned early on in the adult practice groups was the importance of providing a variety of "ways in," since individuals focus and relax in different ways (for example, some like music and guidance, while others prefer quiet, and for some, slow movement/stretching or walking is more relaxing than sitting or lying down). For adults and students alike, it is important to honor these personal differences and build in some flexibility and accommodations/choices where possible.

The majority of students were very receptive and seemed to enjoy the quieting lessons and practices. Teachers appreciated the sense of calm that ensued. At Lantieri's suggestion, many teachers created "peace corners" in their classroom, where students were allowed to go for periods of time to calm themselves as needed. They had various calming tools there for support, such as smooth stones, peaceful nature images, slow gel timers, finger labyrinths, and mandala designs to color. Students often took ownership of these corners in their classrooms and made suggestions for things that would be helpful. One class kept a collective gratitude journal at the peace corner that any student could write in, and another had a miniature Japanese Zen garden.

The program accomplished what we had hoped for at the outset—to address adult and student stress levels and provide support for the existing social and emotional curriculum, Responsive Classroom, without increasing demands on teachers. It was not a separate add-on curriculum, but rather provided complementary, research-based, stress-management tools that could be easily and organically integrated into what teachers were already doing with their students. In many cases, it was as basic as simply remembering to pause for quiet reflection and take deep breaths more often.

At this writing, we are in our second year of the pilot and had a great response to the second introductory training course that Lantieri held in May 2009. We have at least half of the current group wanting to do another year's training to deepen their skills, and a group of about fifty new K–12 participants interested in receiving their first tier of training for the next school year. The plan for the coming year is to build training capacity in our district by having the K–12 guidance team trained to be coaches who can demonstrate IRP classroom activities for teachers. We have applied to various nonprofits for grant funding and are hopeful that in the future, as it becomes more established in the district, the program will become further integrated into the district budget. As a staff member recently said, "This work is too important to be left behind."

RESOURCES

Self-esteem/Self-acceptance

Bruins, D., & H. Leung. *The Legend of Ninja Cowboy Bear*. China: Sure Print & Design, 2008.

Cocca-Leffler, M. *Jack's Talent*. New York: Farrar, Straus & Giroux, 2007.

Dyer, W. W., and K. Tracy. *Incredible You*. Carlsbad, CA: Hay House, 2005.

Dylan, B., and P. Rogers. *Forever Young*. New York: Atheneum Books for Young Readers, 2008.

Livingston, I. *Finklehopper Frog*. Berkeley, CA: Tricycle Press, 2003.

Otoishi, K. *One*. San Rafael, CA: KO Kids Books, 2008.

Rosenthal, A., and T. Lichtenheld. *The OK Book*. New York: HarperCollins, 2007.

Rylant, C., and C. Dowley. *The Wonderful Happens*. New York: Aladdin Paperbacks, 2000.

Seuss, Dr. *Did I Ever Tell You How Lucky You Are?* New York: Random House, 1973.

Self-regulation

Carle, E. *From Head to Toe*. New York: HarperCollins, 1997.

———. *"Slowly, Slowly, Slowly," Said the Sloth*. New York: Puffin Books, 2002.

Churchill, V., and C. Fuge. *Sometimes I Like to Curl Up in a Ball*. New York: Sterling, 2001.

D'Aulaire, I., and E. P. D'Aulaire. *The Two Cars*. New York: New York Review Books, 2007.

Gravett, E. *Monkey and Me*. London: Macmillan Children's Books, 2007.

Pandell, K. *Animal Action ABC*. New York: Dutton Children's Books, 1996.

Rosen, M., and H. Oxenbury. *We're Going on a Bear Hunt*. New York: Aladdin Paperbacks, 1989.

Tankard, J. *Grumpy Bird*. New York: Scholastic Press, 2007.

Books for Teaching Breath Focus/Relaxation

Lite, L. *A Boy and a Bear, the Children's Relaxation Book*. Plantation, FL: Specialty Press, 1996.

MacLean, K. L. *Peaceful Piggy Meditation*. Morton Grove, IL: Albert Whitman, 2004.

———. *Peaceful Piggy Yoga*. Morton Grove, IL: Morton Whitman, 2008.

Susan, S. *Each Breath a Smile*. Berkeley, CA: Parallax Press, 2001.

Urban, L., and H. Cole. *Mouse Was Mad*. New York: Harcourt Children's Books, 2009.

Williams, M. L. *Cool Cats, Calm Kids: Relaxation and Stress Management for Young People*. Atascadero, CA: Impact, 2005.

Feelings/Perspective Taking

Andreae, G. *Keep Love in Your Heart, Little One*. Wilton, CT: Tiger Tales, 2006.

Bang, M. *When Sophie Gets Angry—Really, Really Angry*. New York: Scholastic Press, 1999.

Burningham, J. *John Patrick Norman McHennessy: The Boy Who Was Always Late*. New York: Alfred A. Knopf, 1987.

Cave, K., and N. Maland. *You've Got Dragons*. Atlanta: Peachtree, 2003.

Charlip, R. *Fortunately.* New York: Simon & Schuster, 1993.

Curtis, J. L. *Today I Feel Silly, and Other Moods That Make My Day.* New York: HarperCollins, 1998.

Cuyler, M. *That's Good, That's Bad.* New York: Henry Holt, 1991.

Demi. *The Girl Who Drew a Phoenix.* New York: Margaret K. McElderderry Books, 2008.

Dengler, M. *The Worry Stone.* Flagstaff, AZ: Northland, 1996.

Frame, J. A. *Yesterday I Had the Blues.* Berkeley, CA: Tricycle Press, 2003.

Frasier, D. *On the Day You Were Born.* New York: Harcourt Brace, 1991.

Giovanni, N. *Hip Hop Speaks to Children.* Naperville, IL: Sourceworks Jabberwocky, 2008.

Goldblatt, R. *The Boy Who Didn't Want to be Sad.* Washington, DC: Magination Press, 2004.

Gravett, E. *Little Mouse's Big Book of Fears.* London: Macmillan Children's Books, 2007.

Henkes, K. *A Good Day.* New York: HarperCollins, 2007.

Jeffers, O. *Lost and Found.* New York: HarperCollins, 2005.

Jenkins, E. *The Little Bit Scary People.* New York: Hyperion Books for Children, 2008.

Karst, P. *The Invisible String.* Camarillo, CA: DeVorss, 2000.

Lear, E. *The Owl and the Pussycat.* Tonowanda, NY: Kinds Can Press, 2007.

MacDonald, M. R. *Peace Tales: World Folktales to Talk About.* Hamden, CT: Linnet Books, 1992.

Moser, A. *Don't Pop Your Cork on Mondays!* Kansas City, MO: Landmark Editions, 1998.

Parr, T. *The Feel Good Book.* New York: Little, Brown, 2002.

Penner, F. *Proud.* Marietta, GA: Longstreet Press, 1997.

Sederman, M., and S. Epstein. *The Magic Box: When Parents Can't Be There to Tuck You In.* Washington, DC: Magination Press, 2003.

Spelman, C. M. *When I Feel Angry.* Morton Grove, IL: Albert Whitman, 2000.

Seuss, Dr. *My Many Colored Days.* New York: Random House, 1996.

Tankard, J. *Boo Hoo Bird.* New York: Scholastic Press, 2009.

Teckentrup, B. *Grumpy Cat.* New York: Boxer Books, 2008.

Waber, B. *Courage.* Boston: Houghton Mifflin, 2002.

Watt, M. *Scaredy Squirrel Makes a Friend.* Tonawanda, NY: Kids Can Press, 2007.

Webster, N. J. *The Gift of You, the Gift of Me.* Rochester, NY: StarMist Books, 2005.

Wolff, F., and H. M. Savitz. *Is a Worry Worrying You?* Terre Haute, IN: Tanglewood Press, 2007.

Yashima, T. *Crow Boy.* New York: Puffin Books, 1983.

Young, E. *Seven Blind Mice.* New York: Philomel Books, 1992.

Nature/Compassion/Relationship

Anthony, J. *The Dandelion Seed.* Nevada City, CA: Dawn, 1997.

Asch, F. *The Earth and I.* New York: Harcourt Brace, 1994.

Barbey, B. *Meow Said the Mouse.* Berkeley, CA: Plum Blossom Books, 2005.

Bauer, J. *Selma.* La Jolla, CA: Kane/Miller, 2002.

Baylor, B. *Everybody Needs a Rock.* New York: Aladdin Paperbacks, 1974.

———. *I'm in Charge of Celebrations.* New York: Aladdin Paperbacks, 1974.

———. *The Other Way to Listen.* New York: Aladdin Paperbacks, 1986.

———. *The Way to Start a Day.* New York: Aladdin Paperbacks, 1977.

Boritzer, E. *What Is Beautiful?* Santa Monica, CA: Veronica Lane Books, 2002.

Bunting, E. *Secret Place.* New York: Clarion Books, 1996.

Cooper, I. *The Golden Rule.* New York: Harry N. Abrams, 2007.

Emberley, B., and E. Emberley. *Night's Nice.* New York: Little, Brown, 2008.

Goodall, J. *The Eagle and the Wren.* New York: North-South Books, 2000.

Johnson, D. B. *Henry Builds a Cabin.* Boston: Houghton Mifflin, 2002.

———. *Henry Climbs a Mountain.* Boston: Houghton Mifflin, 2003.

———. *Henry Hikes to Fitchburg.* Boston: Houghton Mifflin, 2006.

———. *Henry Works.* Boston: Houghton Mifflin, 2004.

Joosse, B. *In the Night Garden.* New York: Henry Holt, 2008.

Liao, J. *The Blue Stone: A Journey through Life.* New York: Little, Brown, 2008.

London, J. *Dream Weaver.* New York: Harcourt, 1998.

MacLachlan, P. *All the Places to Love.* New York: HarperCollins, 1994.

Mason, M. *Inside All.* New York: Dawn, 2008.

Mazer, A. *The Salamander Room.* New York: Dragonfly Books, 1991.

Muth, J. J. *The Three Questions.* New York: Scholastic Press, 2002.

———. *Zen Shorts.* New York: Scholastic Press, 2005.

Nash, M. R. *There Is a Tree.* Burlington, VT: Blue Barn Books, 2007.

Park, T. *The Peace Book.* New York: Little, Brown, 2004.

Paulsen, R. W. *The Tortilla Factory.* New York: Harcourt Brace, 1995.

Pendell, K. *By Day and by Night.* Tiburon, CA: H. J. Kramer, 2001.

A Precious Life. Berkeley, CA: Dharma, 1991. [CD, 2001].

Prevert, J., and M. Gersteub. *How to Paint the Portrait of a Bird.* New York: Roaring Brook Press, 2007.

Rylant, C., and N. McClure. *All in a Day.* New York: Abrams Books for Young Readers, 2009.

Susan, S. *The Sun in My Belly.* Berkeley, CA: Plum Blossom Books, 2007.

Tillman, N., and E. Metaxas. *It's Time to Sleep, My Love.* New York: Felwel & Friends, 2008.

The Value of Friends. Berkeley, CA: Dharma, 1991. [CD, 2002].

Waddell, M. *Can't You Sleep, Little Bear?* Boston: Walker Books, 1998.

Wallace, N. E. *The Kindness Quilt.* Tarrytown, NY: Marshall Cavendish, 2006.

A Wise Ape Teaches Kindness. Berkeley, CA: Dharma, 1999.

Zolotow, C. *If You Listen.* Philadelphia: Running Press, 2002.

———. *When the Wind Stops.* New York: HarperCollins, 1995.

Yoga/Relaxation Books, Manuals, & Videos

Allen, J. S., and R. J. Klein. *Ready, Set, Relax: A Research-Based Program of Relaxation, Learning, and Self-esteem for Children.* Watertown, WI: Inner Coaching, 1996.

Belknap, M. *Stress Relief for Kids: Taming Your Dragons.* Duluth, MN: Whole Person Associates, 2006.

Bersma, D., and M. Visscher. *Yoga Games for Children*. Berkeley, CA: Hunter House, 2003.

Caldwell, M. *The Girls Yoga Book*. Berkeley, CA: Maple Tree Press, 2005.

Children of Yogaville. *Hatha Yoga for Kids by Kids!* Buckingham, VA: Integral Yoga, 1990.

Cohen, K. K. *Imagine That! A Child's Guide to Yoga*. Buckingham, VA: Integral Yoga, 1983.

Crist, J. J. *What to Do When You're Sad and Lonely*. Minneapolis, MN: Free Spirit, 2006.

———. *What to Do When You're Scared and Worried*. Minneapolis, MN: Free Spirit, 2004.

Dass, B. H. *A Child's Garden of Yoga*. Santa Cruz, CA: Sri Rama, 1980.

De Brunhoff, L. *Babar's Yoga for Elephants*. New York: Harry N. Abrams, 2002.

Fugitt, E. D. *He Hit Me Back First!* Long Beach, CA: Jalmar Press, 1973.

Garth, M. *Earthlight: New Meditations for Children*. New York: HarperCollins, 1997.

———. *Moonbeam: A Book of Meditations for Children*. New York: HarperCollins, 1992.

———. *Starbright: Meditations for Children*. New York: HarperCollins, 1991.

Kalish, L., and D. Spahn. *Yoga Kit Instruction Book*. Pacific Palisades, CA: Imaginazium, 2000.

Kreidler, W. *Creative Conflict Resolution*. Glenview, IL: Good Year Books, 1984.

Lesky, A. (Producer), and T. Landon (Director). *Yoga Fitness for Kids* [Motion picture]. Louisville, CO: Gaiam, n.d.

Maxwell, R., M. Thomas, and R. Paula (Producers). *EIEI Yoga* [Motion picture]. New York: Mystic Fire Video, 1996.

McKay, M., and P. Fanning. *The Daily Relaxer*. Oakland, CA: New Harbinger, 1997.

Mendler, A. N. *Smiling at Yourself*. Santa Cruz, CA: Network Publications, 1990.

Meyer, F. *Meditations for Children*. [CD]. Worcester, MA: Center for Mindfulness in Medicine, Health Care, and Society, 2004.

Murdock, M. *Spinning Inward*. Boston: Shambhala, 1987.

Nadeau, K. G., and E. B. Dixon. *Learning to Slow Down and Pay Attention: A Book for Kids about ADHD* (3rd ed.). Washington, DC: Magination Press, 2005.

Nhat Hanh, T. (Producer). *Mindful Movements* [Motion picture]. Boulder, CO: Sounds True, 1998.

Quintin, J. *Mandala Coloring Book*. Carlsbad, CA: Hay House, 1998.

Reiner, T., and W. Reiner. *Yoga for Cats*. New York: St. Martin's Paperback, 1989.

Solis, S. *Storytime Yoga: Teaching Yoga to Children through Story*. Boulder, CO: Mythis Yoga Studio, 2006.

Stewart, M. *Yoga for Children*. New York: Simon & Schuster, 1992.

Wenig, M. (Director). *Yoga Kids* [Motion picture]. New Buffalo, MI: TM Books and Video, 1996.

Williams, M. S., and S. Shellenberger. *"How Does Your Engine Run?" A Leader's Guide to the Alert Program for Self-Regulation*. Albuquerque, NM: TherapyWorks, 1996.

———. *Take Five! Staying Alert at Home and School*. Albuquerque, NM: TherapyWorks, 2001.

REFERENCES

Baylor, B., & Parnall, P. (1978). *The other way to listen.* New York: Charles Scribner's Sons.

Carle, E. (2002). *"Slowly, slowly, slowly," said the sloth.* New York: Puffin Books.

Charlip, R. (1993). *Fortunately.* New York: Simon & Schuster.

Committee for Children. (2010). *Second step.* www.cfchildren.org/programs/ssp/overview/.

Iacoboni, Marco. 2008. Mirroring People: The Science of Empathy and How We Connect with Others. New York: Picador/Farrar, Straus and Giroux.

Cuyler, M. (1991). *That's good, that's bad.* New York: Henry Holt.

Johnson, D. B. (2002). *Henry builds a cabin.* Boston: Houghton Mifflin.

———. (2003). *Henry climbs a mountain.* Boston: Houghton Mifflin.

———. (2006). *Henry hikes to Fitchburg.* Boston: Houghton Mifflin.

Lantieri, L. (2008). *Building emotional intelligence: Techniques to cultivate inner strength in children.* Boulder, CO: Sounds True.

Lions Quest. (2011). *Skills for growing.* www.lions-quest.org/skillsgrow.php.

Northeast Foundation for Children. (2010). *Responsive classroom.* www.responsive classroom.org.

Ramachandran, V. S. 2000. "Mirror neurons and imitation learning as the driving force behind 'the Great Leap Forward' in human evolution," Edge 69, June 29, 2000. www.edge.org/3rd_culture/ramachandran/ramachandran_index.html.

Tankard, J. (2007). *Grumpy Bird.* New York: Scholastic Press.

Williams, M. S., & Shellenberger, S. (1996). *"How does your engine run?" A leader's guide to the ALERT program for self-regulation.* Albuquerque, NM: TherapyWorks.

Conclusion

Aostre N. Johnson and Marilyn Webb Neagley

We hope that this book will be a valuable addition to the literature on educating with heart and spirit, especially in the ways that this perspective can be actively used in K–12 educational settings. We believe that each author has contributed valuable insights based on his or her own understanding and experiences. The process of listening to teachers who encourage heart-centered education has been informative. We have learned many lessons not only from the written chapters but also from encouraging the university classes and school-wide initiatives, which resulted in the varied chapters. These lessons include the following.

The Importance of Language

The language that is used to describe this kind of work is critical and will be unique to each setting. Each educator will need to find appropriate words to communicate what he or she means by "educating from the heart" in order to avoid alienating parents and colleagues. In public schools, the language must not connote specific religions or doctrines or seem too soft, or "touchy-feely," as some might say. This is a delicate issue that may require some trial, error, and correction, as well as courage on the part of educators. It may not be possible to please everyone, but the potential benefits are so great that the effort is worth the risks.

The Significance of Starting with Teachers and Administrators

Ideally, educators will begin the process of educating with heart and spirit with *themselves*, or at least they will enter into it as they introduce these methods to children and adolescents. The personal presence and atmosphere that educators bring to the classroom sets the tone for relationships with students, the quality of learning overall, and the success of specific heart and spirit lessons and exercises. The great variety of methods available for educators to work on their own calming, centering, reflecting, focusing, connecting, and so forth is suggested in many of the chapters in this book. Time for educator retreats of varying lengths, from dedicated daily time to longer intentional time away to focus on the inner life, is very supportive for strengthening these initiatives.

The Benefits of Administrative Support

Decades of research demonstrate that any new addition to the curriculum is much more likely to be implemented in a sustained way if it has administrative support. This book is intended for both administrators and teachers, and our hope is that some administrators will initiate school-wide programs that address heart and spirit, which can be embraced by everyone or can be entered into by teachers on a voluntary basis. Research also tells us that coercion is usually counterproductive, but that administrative support can reap impressive benefits. Necessary types of support include enthusiasm and interest, material resources, and long-term professional development opportunities.

The Benefits of Collegial Support and the Potential for Individual Efforts

As suggested above, it seems that this kind of work is most effective when teams of teachers—if not the entire faculty of a school or district—voluntarily engage in a joint educational initiative led or backed by administrators. However, even if the initiative is not school-wide, many other kinds of collegial support are possible and helpful. The chapters written by teachers and counselors in this book describe their own individual work, but each writer had some kind of group support. For example, seven of them were involved with university courses related to teaching with spirit. The two school counselors became involved with a district-wide program. The health educators at one high school all agreed to embrace the same initiative.

Even without group support, individual teachers are encouraged to introduce this work into their classrooms. The "ripple effect" is a key idea here. One teacher supporting one group of children can accomplish much—and when other teachers notice positive impacts on students, they may become interested in learning about the methods.

The Importance of Incorporating This Kind of Work into Higher Education Classes

A number of the K–12 educators represented in this book wrote their chapters while enrolled in higher education classes on "educating from the heart." Many graduate courses relating to heart- and spirit-based methods of education are being offered across the world, and this seems to be a growing trend. When teachers study these methods in a course rooted in the latest literature and research, with support from both the professor and other students, they often feel more empowered to incorporate them into their classrooms and to explain their rationale to administrators, peers, and parents.

In addition, increasingly, professors in colleges and universities are introducing heart/spirit theory and practice in undergraduate and postgraduate teacher preparation courses. As a result, these approaches are being woven into the lives and instructional methods of teachers of all disciplines and developmental levels at the initial stages. Because this book is accessible to educators at various stages and includes both theory and practice, we believe that professors will easily be able to incorporate it into a variety of curriculum and teaching courses. They could experiment with methods in college classes first, so that aspiring educators become familiar and comfortable with using them in their own lives and learning before integrating them into their classroom practices.

The Comparative Benefits of Educator Created vs. "School-Ready" Curricula

There is a long debate in the history of education about the value of prewritten curricula. However, a wide variation exists within this genre. "Teacher-proof" curricula intended to be followed as a rigid script or recipe are obviously anti-intellectual and can be as numbing and alienating as the current "teach to the test" movement referred to in the introduction. However, purchased curricula are not all highly prescriptive; many are useful as resource guides and starting points for lesson planning.

One example of a rich heart-centered curriculum, Linda Lantieri's Inner Resilience Program, is referenced in the final chapter written by Auriel Gray; she also discusses a district-wide voluntary initiative to implement it. Obviously, a school or district implementation process is more efficient if there is an agreed-upon curriculum. Many of the chapters in this book offer fertile resource guides or individual units of study that could easily be adapted for implementation into varied settings. On the other end of the spectrum, there are great benefits in terms of "ownership" to teachers working together to create their own curriculum. This book could serve as a useful starting place for a group of educators to begin their own process of creation of a curriculum that is ideally suited to their interests and needs.

The Varied Content and Methods of Curricular Approaches to Educating with Heart and Spirit

As illustrated in this book, there are a variety of approaches and methods related to the broad initiative of educating with heart and spirit. Some of these include teacher presence and connections with students, self-reflection, regular quiet times, deep listening to music or nature sounds, yoga, mindfulness exercises, classroom rituals, emotional education, carefully selected children's literature and discussion, in-depth reflection on topics of student interest, reflective writing, utilization of all forms of artistic expression, humor, and outdoor exploration. It is critical to keep in mind that valid educational methods in this arena are vast and evolving. Educators will explore and experiment with the most appropriate for themselves, their settings, and their students.

Benefits to Varying Ages or Grades of Students

These methods can be introduced at any age or grade, from young children through adolescents, as this book describes. When students are engaged in these kinds of activities at the earlier stages, they are very open and accepting. Young children become accustomed to and enjoy sitting in silence and focusing on their breathing for gradually lengthening periods of time. Older students may have to be convinced over time of its benefits, but ample evidence is presented in this book that they can be persuaded. As discussed in Sue Wood and Deb Higgins's chapter, adolescents were generally responsive to the concepts of both stress reduction and reflective, philosophical discourse.

The Importance of Including Parents

Parental support is gained when educators explain their curriculum to parents in language that makes sense to them. Supportive parents encourage teachers to proceed with this curriculum and help to reinforce the learning at home. It is possible to include parents through such activities as book groups on related topics, parent–child retreats or programs, and school reading programs.

The Need for Research and Funding

Although there is a long historical tradition of educating with heart and spirit, this has not been the prevailing approach in the modern era, and it has been in steep decline for at least the last decade. There is a current resurgence of interest in these approaches, in opposition to the dominant trend. To become convinced of its value, many people require proof of its effectiveness. Some of the chapters in this book, including Anthony Quintiliani's, highlight recent research results. Funding for further research seems necessary to boost these approaches into mainstream education.

Funding is also needed to produce and publish more curricular resources in this area and to educate consultants who could provide professional development to schools. In addition, school- and district-wide initiatives require financial support to purchase materials, educate teachers about available resources, and provide time for them to work on developing and integrating curricula. We hope that a variety of private and public funding will become available to encourage and sustain these efforts.

The editors of this book hope that it will encourage a wide variety of support for educating with heart and spirit. We believe that the impact of these educational efforts represents healing and a brighter future for youth and the world they are inheriting. In the words of Steven Glazer (1999): "The heart of learning is returning to the heart of all of life. The heart of life is openness, awareness and wholeness inseparable" (p. 250).

REFERENCE

Glazer, S. (Ed.). (1999). *The heart of learning: Spirituality in education.* New York: J. P. Tarcher/Putnam.

Biographical Sketches

Shown in Order of Appearance

Paul D. Houston, Ph.D., currently serves as president of the Center for Empowered Leadership. He is also executive director emeritus of the American Association of School Administrators (AASA), having previously served for more than fourteen years as its executive director. Houston has received numerous honors, including, in 2008, the prestigious American Education Award from AASA and, in 2009, the Learning and Liberty Award from the National School Public Relations Association. Dr. Houston's extensive writing includes more than 250 articles in various professional magazines and journals, and he has coauthored three books: *Exploding the Myths* (1993), *The Board-Savvy Superintendent* (2003), and *The Spiritual Dimension of Leadership* (2006).

Marilyn Webb Neagley is coordinator of the Talk About Wellness initiative. She has worked both locally and nationally for the past forty years with non-profit organizations as a CEO, volunteer, board member, and/or consultant. She was most recently the recipient of an IPPY gold medal for best Northeastern nonfiction for her book of reflections, *Walking through the Seasons*.

Aostre N. Johnson, Ed.D., is professor of education at Saint Michael's College in Colchester, Vermont. She teaches courses in integrated curriculum theory and practice and child development in education, and she directs a master's program in curriculum. She has published many articles related to creativity, ethics, spirituality, religion, human development, and education and is a coeditor of *Nurturing Child and Adolescent Spirituality: Perspectives from the World's Religious Traditions.* She has also cofounded and directed holistic schools for children.

Tobin Hart, Ph.D., is a father, teacher, author, and psychologist. He serves as professor of psychology at the University of West Georgia. He is cofounder of the ChildSpirit Institute, a nonprofit educational and research hub exploring and nurturing the spirituality of children and adults. His work examines consciousness, spirituality, psychotherapy, and education. His most recent books include *From Information to Transformation: Education for the Evolution of Consciousness* and *The Secret Spiritual World of Children.*

Anthony R. Quintiliani, Ph.D., was the clinical director of a center for mental health and substance abuse services. In his thirty-five years of professional experience, he has also served in public education, higher education, and various clinical consulting roles. He has published articles and handbooks in both clinical psychology and education. Dr. Quintiliani is considered an expert in psychological and organizational aspects of co-occurring disorders and mindfulness implementation in systems.

Ann Trousdale, Ed.D., is an associate professor at Louisiana State University, where she teaches courses in children's literature, language arts, and storytelling. Her research interests include reader response to literature; theological, sociopolitical, and feminist analysis of children's literature; the oral interpretation of literature; and using literature to support children's spiritual lives and religious understanding. She is also an ordained deacon in the United Methodist Church.

Rachael Kessler is the founder and president of the PassageWorks Institute and the author of *The Soul of Education*: *Helping Students Find Connection, Compassion and Character at School* (2000) and coauthor of *Promoting Social and Emotional Learning: Guidelines for Educators* (1997). She published widely in the fields of social and emotional learning, transformative learning, teacher education, spirituality in education, and holistic education. She also offered keynotes, professional development, and consulting nationally and internationally.

Laura Weaver, M.A., has worked for fifteen years in the fields of education and social service, joining the PassageWorks Institute in 2003. As director of programs, she writes curriculum and serves as the lead faculty member providing professional development and presentations for teachers and overseeing PassageWorks faculty. She is also a published poet and essayist and facilitator of rites-of-passage work with girls and women.

Peter Perkins, M.A., is the principal learning consultant, coach, and teacher with Five Dimensions of Calais, Vermont, facilitating adolescent learning and holistic development, with an emphasis on spiritual growth. He is also senior associate and partner with Global Learning Partners, Inc., teaching dialogue education since 1985. He has authored, coauthored, or contributed to works on dialogue education, adolescent spirituality, and youth substance abuse intervention and prevention.

Jacqueline Kaufman, M.A., is a licensed English and special education teacher who also holds Highly Qualified Teacher certification in social studies. She is a sixteen-year veteran of alternative education programs. She earned her master's in contemplative education in 2007 and became an adjunct instructor in the Saint Michael's College (Vermont) Graduate Program in Education in 2008.

Donald Tinney wrote his first book, *Vermonters*, in 1985. Since then, he has contributed articles and chapters to various publications, including *Vermont Life*, *The Vermont Encyclopedia*, and *The Relevance of English*. He served as president of the Vermont Council of Teachers of English from 1994 until 1998; he also served on the board of directors of the National Council of Teachers of English for four years.

Sara Caldwell teaches middle school in Montgomery Center, Vermont. She has been working with children for the past fifteen years, both in a school and in wilderness programs.

Joyce Kemp, M.A., is the digital arts instructor at a technical center and also teaches at a community college. She has been involved with education for twenty-five years.

Sue Wood, M.A., has taught high school health and physical education for twenty-four years. She has helped develop a comprehensive personal fitness course required for all of the school's graduates, integrating yoga and mindfulness techniques into her teachings.

Deb Higgins has been a wellness teacher for over thirty years. In addition to serving as a representative of the National Honor Society Faculty Committee and the Freshmen Core Program, she is a member of the State and National Alliances for Health, PE, Recreation, and Dance.

Deborah Thomsen-Taylor, M.A., has taught middle school language arts and social studies for fifteen years and is a nationally board-certified social studies teacher.

Jessica Toulis has taught for eight years at the elementary school level and is currently teaching at the Shelburne Community School in Shelburne, Vermont.

Madelyn Nash, M.A., is a school counselor working with third through fifth graders in South Burlington, Vermont. She has been an educator and counselor for more than thirty years and has worked in the areas of conflict resolution and peer mediation. She finds the strategies of calming the body and focusing the mind essential in helping students build emotional intelligence.

Auriel Gray, MACP, CYT, is a school counselor in Vermont at an elementary school where she has worked for twenty-five years. She is also a certified yoga teacher and enjoys exploring the mind-body-spirit-world connection with students and sharing holistic approaches to learning and wellness with her teaching colleagues.